Phr...

PORTUGUESE

With menu decoder, survival guide and two-way dictionary

Thomas Cook
Publishing

www.thomascookpublishing.com

Introduction......................5

Greetings..........................9

Eating out......................13

Shopping..........................29

Getting around..............37

Accommodation..............43

Survival guide..................49

Emergencies.....................59

Dictionary........................63

Quick reference................95

How to use this guide

The ten chapters in this guide are colour-coded to help you find what you're looking for. These colours are used on the tabs of the pages and in the contents on the opposite page and above.

For quick reference, you'll find some basic expressions on the inside front cover and essential emergency phrases on the inside back cover. There is also a handy reference section for numbers, measurements and clothes sizes at the back of the guide.

Front cover photography by Richard Klune/Corbis
Cover design/artwork by Sharon Edwards
Photos: Nara Vieira da Silva Osga (p24), Kristin Smith (p31),
Pasqualantonio Pingue (p43), Pedro Valdeolmillos (p49), Ronaldo
Taveira (p50) and Nuno Ribeiro (p58).

Produced by The Content Works Ltd
www.thecontentworks.com
Design concept: Mike Wade
Layout: Tika Stefano
Text: Peter Wise
Editing: Rachel Fell & Amanda Castleman
Proofing: Wendy Janes
Project editor: Begoña Juarros
Management: Lisa Plumridge & Rik Mulder

Published by Thomas Cook Publishing
A division of Thomas Cook Tour Operations Limited
Company Registration No. 1450464 England
PO Box 227, Unit 18, Coningsby Road
Peterborough PE3 8SB, United Kingdom
email: books@thomascook.com
www.thomascookpublishing.com
+ 44 (0)1733 416477

ISBN-13: 978-184157-675-6

First edition © 2007 Thomas Cook Publishing
Text © 2007 Thomas Cook Publishing

Project Editor: Kelly Pipes
Production/DTP: Steven Collins

Printed and bound in Italy by Printer Trento

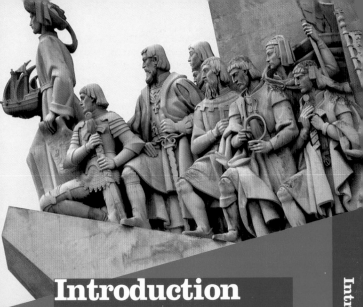

Introduction

Bossa nova, cobra, marmalade, monsoon, molasses and teak. See? You already know a lot of Portuguese, since English poached some of its terms. The language descends from Latin, but has a strong Arabic influence (particularly words beginning with "al-"), as a result of the Moorish occupation of the Iberian peninsula during the Middle Ages.

Portuguese navigators, like Vasco da Gama, spread the tongue across the world. It remains the official language of former colonies, such as Angola, Brazil and Mozambique. Any skill you gain is useful, as – together with Spanish – it's the fastest growing western language.

The basics

Portuguese, the sixth most widely used language in the world, is spoken by more than 220 million people in countries including Brazil and Angola. A romance language based on Latin, it is grammatically akin to French and resembles Spanish on the page. Anyone who can read Spanish can fake through Portuguese text. But the sounds are very different. Without prior study, most Portuguese can understand clearly spoken Spanish. But the Spanish can't easily comprehend Portuguese, mainly due to pronunciation differences.

Particularly distinctive qualities of Portuguese include the endings -ão and -ões. Say these with a nasal twang, like the -own in "frown" and -oings in "boings" (imagine the sound of a bouncing ball). An **s** at the end of a word or before a consonant is usually pronounced "sshh". The letter **x** is also pronounced "sshh". This lends a general "shushing" sound, which many find similar to Slavic languages. Native speakers also run words together and tend not to enunciate endings clearly. This, rather than grammar or vocabulary, gives Portuguese a reputation as a tough language.

This small country has always lived in the shadow of a more powerful neighbour. Though friendly and hospitable, its people firmly maintain the distinctions between the two countries. If you can't speak the native tongue, try English rather than Spanish to avoid offence.

Portuguese uses four accents, which are an important guide to pronunciation. The general rule is to exaggerate the second-to-last syllable (for example, **socorro** – help! – sounds like *soocorroo*; **aberto** – open – sounds like *abairto*). Three accents – ´, ^ and ˜ – indicate stresses elsewhere.

Like other Latin-based languages, Portuguese assigns genders to nouns. Use the corresponding definite articles to say "the": "**o**" for masculine words and "**a**" for feminine. The indefinite article "a" is "**um**" (m) and "**uma**" (f).

Adjectives must match the gender of the thing they describe. Add **-o** to the end of masculine terms, **-a** to feminine.

Verbs conjugate like those in French and Spanish, revealing who did what – and when. The Portuguese often don't use pronouns with verbs, saying, for example, just **vejo** rather than **eu vejo** for "I see".

Top marks for effort

The Portuguese are good linguists and English is widespread. However, they are very appreciative when foreigners make the effort to converse in their native tongue. Unless you're a Spaniard, it's better to avoid Spanish.

As in most Latin-based languages, there are two verbs for the English verb "to be": **ser** and **estar**. The Portuguese use **ser** to describe the essence of something, or how a thing is always – for example: **Sou de Londres** (I'm from London). They use **estar** to describe how someone or something is at the moment – for example: **Estou cansado** (I'm tired).

English and Portuguese share quite a few similar terms. Sometimes you can guess a word just by adding "**o**" or "**a**". But that tactic can also go horribly wrong. Here are some "false friends": words that resemble each other, but express very different ideas:

Puxe – pull (not push)
Assistir – to attend (not to assist)
Balcão – a bank or café counter (not a balcony)
Cigarro – cigarette (not cigar)
Constipado – to have a cold (not to be constipated)
Simpático – nice (not sympathetic)
Petróleo – oil (not petrol)
Livraria – bookshop (not library)

Accents vary from region to region and can be particularly tricky in the islands of Madeira and the Azores. The dialects in Portugal and Brazil differ much like British English and the American variety.

7

Most foreigners find Brazilian Portuguese easier to understand.

Today, the language thrives from Macau in China to the Caribbean and Africa, often in a creole form. Many people consider it the most melodic Western tongue – and its nicknames include "the last flower of Latium" and "the sweet language". In 2006, the Museum of Portuguese Language opened in the city with the largest concentration of speakers worldwide: São Paulo, Brazil.

Basic conversation

Hello	**Olá**	_olah_
Goodbye	**Adeus**	_adayoosh_
Yes	**Sim**	_seeng_
No	**Não**	_nowng_
Please	**Por favor**	_pohr favohr_
Thank you	**Obrigado/a**	_ohbreegahdoo/a_
You're welcome	**De nada**	_d nahda_
Sorry	**Desculpe**	_dshcoolp_
Excuse me (apology)	**Desculpe**	_dshcoolp_
Excuse me (to get attention)	**Por favor**	_pohr favohr_
Excuse me (to get past)	**Com licença**	_cong leesengsa_
Do you speak English?	**Fala inglês?**	_fahla eenglaysh?_
I don't speak Portuguese	**Não falo português**	_nowng fahloo portoogaysh_
I speak a little Portuguese	**Falo um pouco português**	_fahloo oong pohkoo portoogaysh_
What?	**O que?**	_oo k?_
I understand	**Entendo**	_entehndoo_
I don't understand	**Não entendo**	_nowng entehndoo_
Do you understand?	**Entende?**	_entehnd?_
I don´t know	**Não sei**	_nowng say_
I can´t	**Não posso**	_nowng pohssoo_
Can you... please?	**Pode... por favor?**	_pohd... pohr favohr?_
- speak more slowly	**- falar mais devagar**	_- fahlar mayeesh dehvahgar_
- repeat that	**- repetir isso**	_- rehpeteer eessoo_

Greetings

The Portuguese are friendly and
hospitable, particularly towards
foreigners. A polite request for help is
almost always honoured.

As a rule, the Portuguese excel at foreign
languages and relish English
conversation. People in the north tend to be
more down-to-earth and outgoing. In the
south, they are more polite and reserved.

Shake hands with everyone, right down to
the smallest toddler, when meeting
or departing, but mind your body
language: pointing is insulting here. Also,
avoid waving. Beckon with your hand
down, as if patting a dog on the head.

Meeting someone

Hello	**Olá**	*ohlah*
Hi	**Olá**	*ohlah*
Good morning	**Bom dia**	*bong deea*
Good afternoon	**Boa tarde**	*boa tard*
Good evening	**Boa noite**	*boa noyt*
Sir/Mr	**Senhor**	*senyoor*
Madam/Mrs	**Senhora**	*senyoora*
Miss	**Menina**	*meneena*
How are you?	**Como está?**	*koomoo ishtah?*
Fine, thank you	**Bem, obrigado**	*beng, ohbreegahdoo*
And you?	**E você?**	*e voosseh?*
Very well	**Muito bem**	*mweetoo beng*
Not very well	**Não muito bem**	*naowng mweetoo beng*

Hugs & kisses

The Portuguese are warm and tactile. Family and friends kiss on both cheeks when they meet. Men always shake hands, and often hug and back-slap too.

Small talk

My name is...	**O meu nome é...**	*oh mayoo nohm eh...*
What's your name?	**Como se chama?**	*koomoo se shahma?*
I'm pleased to meet you	**Muito prazer**	*mweetoo prazayr*

Where are you from?	Donde é?	dongd eh?
I am from Britain	Sou da Grã-bretanha	soou da grang-bre-tanya
Do you live here?	Vive aqui?	veev akee?
This is a great...	Isto é um fantástico...	ishtoo eh oong fan-tasteekoo...
- country	- país	- paeesh
- city/town	- cidade/vila	- seedahd/veela
I'm in... for...	Estou em... durante...	ishtoou eng... doorangt...
- a weekend	- o fim-de-semana	- o fing de semahna
- a week	- uma semana	- oonga semahna
How old are you?	Quantos anos tem?	kwangtoos anoosh teng?
I'm... years old	Tenho... anos	tenyoo... anoosh

Family

This is...	Isto é...	ishtoo eh...
- my husband	- o meu marido	- o mayoo mareedoo
- my wife	- a minha mulher	- a meenya moolyair
- my partner	- o meu parceiro/a minha parceira	- o mayoo parsay-eeroo/ a meenya parsayeera
- my boyfriend/my girlfriend	- o meu namorado/a minha namorada	- o mayoo namoorah-doo/a meenya namoorahdoo
I have...	Tenho...	tenyoo...
- a son	- um filho	- oong feelyoo
- a daughter	- uma filha	- oonga feelya
- a grandson	- um neto	- oong nehtoo
- a granddaughter	- uma neta	- oonga nehta
Do you have...	Tem...	teng...
- children?	- filhos?	- feelyoosh?
- grandchildren?	- netos?	- nehtoosh?
I don't have children	Não tenho filhos	- naowng tenyoo feelyoosh
Are you married?	É casado/a?	eh kazahdoo/a?
I'm...	Sou...	soou...

- single	**- solteiro/a**	- *sool**tay**eeroo/a*
- married	**- casado/a**	- *ka**zah**doo/a*
- divorced	**- divorciado/a**	*deevorseeyahdoo/a*
- widowed	**- viúvo/a**	*vee**oo**voo/a*

Saying goodbye

Goodbye	**Adeus**	*adayoosh*
Good night	**Boa noite**	*boa noyt*
Sleep well	**Durma bem**	*__door__ma beng*
See you later	**Até logo**	*ah__teh__ __loo__goo*
Have a good trip	**Boa viagem**	*boa vee__yah__zheng*
All the best	**Melhores cumprimentos**	*meel__yo__resh koom-pree__meng__toosh*
Have fun	**Divirta-se**	*dee__veer__ta-seh*
Good luck	**Boa sorte**	*boa sorrt*
Keep in touch	**Mantenha-se em contacto**	*mang__ten__ya-seh eng kon__tak__too*
My address is...	**A minha morada é...**	*a __mee__nya moo__rah__da eh...*

Portuguese flower etiquette

The perfect gift for hosts, but a minefield for the uninitiated. Don't give lilies or chrysanthemums: they're used at funerals. Red flowers should also be avoided, as they're a symbol of the revolution. Bring an odd number, but not 13 – it's considered unlucky.

Eating out

Portuguese cuisine – which makes
liberal use of olive oil, garlic, coriander
and parsley – forms part of the
Mediterranean tradition. But explorers
and colonists brought back far-flung
tastes too, such as saffron, cinnamon,
vanilla and chilli peppers. Arab
influences are also strong, especially
in the south.

Portugal remains a sea-faring nation –
the people here eat more fish per capita
than any other Europeans. The most
characteristic local dish is **bacalhau**, or
cod, specifically the dried and salted
variety. Fresh sardines, grilled in the
open air over charcoal, are almost as
popular during the summer months.

Introduction

Portugal is a café and restaurant society. Breakfast – perhaps just a cup of coffee and a croissant – usually is just a quick café stop. Workers prefer a cheap lunch outside the office to a sandwich at their desk. Most social occasions, such as birthdays and anniversaries, are celebrated with dinner at a good restaurant. Prices are very reasonable, especially when compared to Britain.

I'd like...	**Quero...**	_kayroo..._
- a table for two	**- uma mesa para dois**	_- oonga mehsa para doysh_
- a sandwich	**- uma sandes**	_- oonga sandesh_
- a coffee	**- um café**	_- oong kaffeh_
- a tea (with milk)	**- um chá (com leite)**	_- oong sha (kong lay-eet)_
Do you have a menu in English?	**Tem uma ementa em inglês?**	_teng oonga emengda eng eenglaysh?_
The bill, please	**A conta, por favor**	_a kongda, pohr favohr_

You may hear...

Fumador ou não-fumador?	_foomadohr o naowng foomadohr?_	Smoking or non-smoking?
O que é que vai tomar?	_o k eh vy toomar?_	What are you going to have?

The cuisines of Portugal

National specialities

Don't leave without trying **bacalhau**, the dried, salted cod that can be prepared at least a dozen ways. Other delicacies include grilled sardines, available from May to August, as well as fresh fish and shellfish. The country also offers a huge variety of cheeses, hams and spicy, smoked sausages: each region has its own specialities.

Signature dishes
(see the Menu decoder for more dishes)

Caldo verde	_kaldoo vayrd_	Kale, potato, onion and garlic soup
Açorda de marisco	_assoorda d mareeshkoo_	Shellfish with a bread, garlic and coriander soup
Frango à piri-piri	_frangoo a peerree-peerree_	Barbecued chicken with chilli

Cozido à Portuguesa	*koozeedoo a por-toogayza*	Meat, sausages and vegetables served in broth

Alentejo

Bread, pork and olive oil are staples in the Alentejo region, once the country's main producer of grain. Chefs skilfully employ herbs – particularly coriander, thyme, rosemary and basil – to spin sophisticated dishes from the simplest ingredients. The area's wonderful peasant bread appears in soups and stews, or combined with olive oil and garlic beside meat or fish.

Signature dishes
(see the Menu decoder for more dishes)

Sopa alentejana	*soopa alentezhana*	Bread soup with coriander and egg
Porco à alentejana	*pohrkoo ah alentezhana*	Pork and clams
Ensopado de Borrego	*engsoopahdoo d borrehgoo*	Lamb stew
Coelho em vinho	*koelyoo eng veenoo*	Rabbit cooked in wine
Ameixas de Elvas	*amayeeshas d elvash*	Preserved greengages

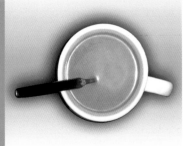

A soup a day...
The Portuguese are big on soup. They often puree vegetables and potatoes into broth. These thick stews are almost complete meals.

Algarve

The Algarve is the place to savour fresh fish and shellfish. Most menus feature tuna steaks, squid, cuttlefish, octopuses and small **carapaus** (a local variety of mackerel). The **cataplana**, a sealed copper pan, produces wonderful fish-and-rice stews. Almonds are blended with egg yolks to make sweet dainties and brewed into **amendoa amarga**, an after-dinner liqueur.

Signature dishes
(see the Menu decoder for more dishes)

Amêijoas na cataplana	*amayeezhoash na kataplana*	Clams cooked in a sealed pan
Atum de cebolada	*atoong d seboolahda*	Tuna with onions and tomatoes
Lulas recheadas	*loolash resheahdash*	Squid stuffed with cured meats
Bolos de massa de amêndoa	*booloosh d massa d amehngdoa*	Marzipan cakes
Figos com amêndoas	*feegoosh kong amehngdoash*	Dried figs studded with almonds

Tipping
The Portuguese tend to round up, rather than calculate percentages. But it is usual to add 5-10% to the price of a meal as a tip.

Central Portugal
Roast suckling pig (**leitão**) – served hot or cold with crisp crackling – is a favourite dish of central Portugal. The Serra da Estrela mountains are also home to **queijo da serra**, a soft, buttery ewe-milk cheese, considered Portugal's best, and most expensive, type. Kid and lamb feature heavily, often spiced with **colorau** (paprika).

Signature dishes
(see the Menu decoder for more dishes)

Sopa de pedra	*soopa d pehdra*	Vegetable and meat soup
Leitão da Bairrada	*layeetaowng da baeerrahda*	Roast suckling pig
Bacalhau à Brás	*bakalyaow ah brash*	Salt cod, potatoes, onion and eggs
Bife à café	*beef a kaffeh*	Steak, creamy sauce, fried egg

Arroz doce	_arrohsh dohss_	Cold rice pudding, lemon and vanilla

Northern Portugal

The cuisine of northern Portugal is the country's richest and most robust. Pride of place goes to **caldo verde**, the nation's signature soup, made from shredded kale, potato and spicy sausage. In the north-east, try a **posta mirandesa**, a steak of local beef. Roast kid (**cabrito assado**) is a favourite in the mountainous interior.

Signature dishes
(see the Menu decoder for more dishes)

Sopa de castanhas	_soopa d kash-tanyash_	Chestnut soup, beans and rice
Feijoada	_fayeezhoahda_	Bean stew, cured meats and rice
Rojões	_rohzhongsh_	Spiced pork in wine and garlic
Morcela	_moorsayla_	Spicy black pudding
Toucinho do céu	_toouseenyoo do seoo_	Rich almond and cinnamon cake

365 Varieties
The Portuguese say there are as many recipes for **bacalhau** (dried, salted cod) as there are days in the year. Whatever the true number, you're unlikely to exhaust the supply on a short holiday.

Madeira
Fish tops the menu on this resort island. **Peixe espada** (scabbard fish) is the most traditional dish, often served with sliced bananas or in a wine-and-vinegar marinade. Another mainstay is **milho frito** (fried maize), an accompaniment to entrees. Tropical fruits grow locally, including passion fruit, mangoes, kiwis, loquat and guava.

Signature dishes
(see the Menu decoder for more dishes)

Sopa de tomate e cebola	_soopa d toomaht e seboola_	Tomato and onion soup
Espetada regional	_ishpetahda rezhional_	Beef kebab
Bacalhau dourado	_bakalyaow doourahda_	Salt cod with eggs and potatoes
Carne de vinho e alhos	_karrn d veenyoo e alyoosh_	Beef in a wine sauce
Bolo do caco	_bohloo do kakoo_	Honey cake

Wine, beer & spirits

Portugal produces many excellent wines, from full-bodied, fruity reds in the Alentejo to light, sparkling **vinho verde** (green wine) in the north-western Minho region. Fortified wines – port – from the Douro valley and Madeira are justly world famous. Grapes also transform into **aguardente**, a brandy, and fiery, clear **bagaceira**.

Vinho verde	_veenyoo vayrd_	Sparkling "green" wine
Vinho do porto	_veenyoo do pohrtoo_	Port wine
Vinho da Madeira	_veenyoo da madayeera_	Madeira wine
Ginginha/Ginja	_zheenzheenya/ zheenya_	Cherry brandy
Amarguinha	_amargheenya_	Almond liqueur

Red, white...or green
Vinho verde means "green wine". But the name refers to the lush vegetation of the Minho region, not to the shade in the glass.

Could I have...?	Posso beber...?	possoo bebayr...?
- a beer	- uma cerveja	- oonga sehrvayzha
- a glass/a bottle of white/red/ rosé wine	- um copo/uma garrafa de vinho branco/tinto/rosé	- oong kopoo/ooma garraffa d veenyoo brangkoo/teeng-too/rohzeh
- a glass/a bottle of champagne	- uma taça/uma garrafa de champanhe	- oonga tassa/ooma garraffa d shampanye
- a gin and tonic	- um gin tónico	- oong zheen tonneekoo
- a rum and coke (Cuba Libre)	- uma Cuba-Livre	- oonga koobah-leevr
- a whisky	- um whisky	- oong weesskee

You may hear...

O que é que posso trazer?	ok eh k possoo trazayr?	What can I get you?
Com ou sem gelo?	kom oh seng zhehloo?	With or without ice?
Fresco ou natural?	freshkoo oh natooral?	Cold or room temperature?

Coffee versus tea

Coffee – usually taken short, strong and black – is an integral part of Portuguese life. Most Brits suffer tea-trauma here: the weak milkless blend is an acquired taste.

Snacks & refreshments

Many cafés are known as **pastelarias**: cake shops. The Portuguese adore sweet pastries and desserts, which are usually based on egg yolks, almonds, cinnamon and lots of sugar. For the ultimate experience, try a **pastel de nata** (custard-cream tartlet), served hot from the oven.

Uma meia de leite	_oonga maya d layeet_	Half coffee, half milk
Um café	_oong kaffeh_	Espresso coffee
Pastel de nata	_pashtel d nahta_	Custard tartlet
Pastel de bacalhau	_pashtel d bakalyaow_	Salt cod savouries
Queijadas de Sintra	_kayeezhadash d seengtra_	Sweet cheese and cinnamon tartlets
Tosta mista	_toshta meeshta_	Toasted cheese and ham sandwich

Vegetarians & special requirements

I'm vegetarian	**Sou vegetariano/a**	_so-ou vezhetareeah-noo/a_
I don't eat...	**Não como...**	_naowng kohmoo..._
- meat	**- carne**	- _karrn_
- fish	**- peixe**	- _payeesh_
I'm allergic...	**Sou alérgico/a...**	_so-ou alayrzheekoo/a..._
- to nuts	**- a nozes**	- _a nohzesh_
- to wheat	**- a trigo**	- _a treegoo_
- to diary	**- ao leite de vaca**	- _ow layeet d vahka_

Children

Are children welcome?	**As crianças são bem vindas?**	_as kreeangsass saowng beng veengdash?_
Do you have a children's menu?	**Tem uma ementa para crianças?**	_teng oonga emengda para kreeangsass?_
Which dishes are good for children?	**Que pratos recomenda para crianças?**	_k prahtoosh rekomengda para kreeangsass?_

Mealtimes

Most restaurants serve lunch from 1pm to 3pm and dinner from 7pm to 10pm.

Menu decoder

Essentials

Breakfast	**Pequeno-almoço**	*pekehnoo-almossoo*
Lunch	**Almoço**	*almossoo*
Dinner	**Jantar**	*zhangtar*
Cover charge	**Couvert**	*koovair*
Vat inclusive	**Inclui iva**	*ingklooi eeva*
Service included	**Serviço incluído**	*serveessoo ingklooeedoo*
Credit cards (not) accepted	**(Não) aceitamos cartões de crédito**	*(naowng) asayeetahmoosh kartongsh d kredeetoo*
First course	**Entrada**	*engtrahda*
Second course	**Prato principal**	*prahtoo preenseepal*
Dessert	**Sobremesa**	*soobremehsa*
Dish of the day	**Prato do dia**	*prahtoo do deea*
House specials	**Pratos da casa**	*prahtoosh da caza*
Set menu	**Ementa fixa**	*emengta feeksa*
A la carte menu	**Ementa a la carte**	*emengta a la karrt*
Tourist menu	**Ementa turística**	*emengta tooreeshteeka*
Wine list	**Lista de vinhos**	*leeshta d veenyoosh*
Drinks menu	**Lista de bebidas**	*leeshta d bebeedash*
Snack menu	**Lista de snacks**	*leeshta d shnaks*

Methods of preparation

Baked	**Assado/a**	*assahdoo/a*
Boiled	**Cosido/a**	*kohzeedoo/a*
Braised	**Estufado/a**	*ishtoofahdoo/a*
Breaded	**Panado**	*panahdoo*
Deep-fried	**Frito/a**	*freetoo/a*
Fresh	**Fresco/a**	*freshkoo/a*
Fried	**Frito/a**	*freetoo/a*
Frozen	**Congelado/a**	*kongzhelahdoo/a*
Grilled/broiled	**Grelhado/a**	*grelyahdoo/a*
Marinated	**Marinado/a**	*mareenahdoo/a*
Mashed	**Esmagado/a**	*ishmagahdoo/a*
Poached	**Escalfado/a**	*ishkalfahdoo/a*
Raw	**Cru/a**	*kroo/a*
Roasted	**Assado/a**	*assahdoo/a*

Light breakfasts

The Portuguese are not big on breakfasts. Few eat eggs or meat. Usually it's just milk, coffee, bread, toast, or a croissant. Fruit juice and breakfast cereals are also common.

Salty	**Salgado/a**	*salgahdoo/a*
Sautéed	**Salteado/a**	*saltayahdoo/a*
Smoked	**Fumado/a**	*foomahdoo/a*
Spicy	**Picante**	*peekangt*
Steamed	**Vaporisado**	*vapohreezahdoo*
Stewed	**Guisado**	*gheezahdoo*
Stuffed	**Recheado/a**	*reshayahdoo/a*
Sweet	**Doce**	*dohss*
Rare	**Mal passado/a**	*mal passahdoo/a*
Medium	**Médio**	*mehdeeo*
Well done	**Bem passado/a**	*beng passahdoo/a*

Common food items

Beef	**Carne de vaca**	*karrn d vakka*
Chicken	**Frango, galinha**	*frangoo, galleenya*
Turkey	**Perú**	*pehroo*
Lamb	**Carne de borrego**	*karrn d borrehgoo*
Pork	**Carne de porco**	*karrn d pohrkoo*
Fish	**Peixe**	*payeesh*
Seafood	**Marisco**	*mareeskoo*
Tuna	**Atum**	*atoong*

Beans	**Feijões**	*fayzhongsh*
Cheese	**Queijo**	*kayeezhoo*
Eggs	**Ovos**	*ohvoosh*
Lentils	**Lentilhas**	*lengteelyash*
Pasta/noodles	**Massa/noodles**	*massa/noodles*
Rice	**Arroz**	*arrosh*
Cabbage	**Couve**	*kohv*
Carrots	**Cenoura**	*senoora*
Cucumber	**Pepino**	*pepeenoo*
Garlic	**Alho**	*alyoo*
Mushrooms	**Cogumelos**	*koogoomehloosh*
Olives	**Azeitonas**	*azayeetoonash*
Onion	**Cebola**	*seboola*
Potato	**Batata**	*batahta*
Red/green pepper	**Pimento vermelho/verde**	*peemengtoo verrmaylyoo/vayrd*
Tomato	**Tomate**	*toomaht*
Vegetables	**Vegetais**	*vezhetaeesh*
Bread	**Pão**	*paowng*
Oil	**Óleo**	*ohlayoo*
Pepper	**Pimenta**	*peemangta*
Salt	**Sal**	*sal*
Vinegar	**Vinagre**	*veenagr*
Cake	**Bolo**	*booloo*
Cereal	**Cereais**	*sere-aeesh*
Cream	**Natas**	*nahtass*
Fruit	**Fruta**	*froota*
Ice-cream	**Gelado**	*zhelahdoo*
Milk	**Leite**	*layeet*
Tart	**Tarte**	*tarrt*

Popular sauces

Molho de tomate	*molyoo d toomaht*	Tomato sauce
Molho de alho	*molyoo d alyoo*	Garlic sauce
Molho de ostras	*molyoo d oshtrash*	Oyster sauce
Vinagrete	*veenagreht*	Vinaigrette
Molho béchamel	*molyoo beshamel*	Béchamel sauce
Molho branco	*molyoo brangkoo*	White sauce with butter and onions
Maionese	*myonehz*	Mayonnaise
Molho inglês	*molyoo eenglaysh*	Worcester sauce

| Escabeche | ishkabesh | Spicy sauce for fish |
| Tempero de salada | tengpehroo d salahda | Salad dressing olive oil and vinegar |

First course dishes

Sopa de peixe	sohpa d payeesh	Fish soup
Caldo verde	kaldoo vayrd	Cabbage and potato soup
Canja de galinha	kangzha d galleenya	Chicken soup
Sopa de pedra	sohpa d pehdra	Vegetable and meat soup
Sopa de tomate	sohpa d toomaht	Tomato soup
Sopa de legumes	sohpa d legoomsh	Vegetable soup
Cocktail de gambas	koktel d gangbash	Prawn cocktail
Presunto	prehzoongtoo	Smoked ham

A load of tripe

Tripas à moda do porto (tripe with white beans) is not for the faint-hearted. The dish is said to have originated during a 14th-century siege of Porto, when the city's inhabitants survived on tripe and other offal. People from Porto are still known as **tripeiros**, or tripe-eaters

Melão	melaowng	Melon
Sopa alentejana	sohpa alengtezhana	Bread-based soup with coriander and a poached egg
Amêijoas na cataplana	amayeezhooash na kataplana	Clams cooked in a sealed pan
Sopa de castanhas	sohpa d kash-tanyash	Chestnut soup with beans and rice
Sopa de tomate e cebola	sohpa d toomaht e seboolash	Tomato and onion soup
Chouriço	sho-oureessoo	Smoked pork sausage

Queijo da Ilha	*kayeezhoo da eelya*	Strong cheese from the Azores
Queijo da Serra	*kayeezhoo da sehrra*	Ewe's milk cheese from Serra da Estrela
Paté	*patteh*	pate

Second course dishes

Caldeirada	*kaldayeerahda*	Fish stew
Goraz	*gooraz*	Bream
Iscas marinadas	*ishkash mareenahdash*	Marinated liver
Lulas	*loolash*	Squid
Peixe espada	*payeesh ishpahda*	Scabbard fish
Polvo	*poolvoo*	Octopus
Salsichas	*salseeshash*	Sausages
Tamboril	*tangbohreel*	Monkfish
Cataplana	*kataplana*	Sealed pan for steaming
Cherne	*shehrrn*	Stone bass
Chocos	*shookoosh*	Cuttlefish
Churrasco	*shoorashkoo*	On the spit
Enguias	*engheeash*	Eels
Açorda	*assoorda*	Bread-based stew
Bacalhau	*bakalyaow*	Dried, salted cod
Aves	*ahvesh*	Poultry
Robalo	*roobaloo*	Bass
Pescada	*peshkahdoo*	Hake
Linguado	*leengwahdoo*	Sole
Sável	*sahvel*	Shad
Lampreia	*langpraya*	Lamprey
Salmonete	*salmooneht*	Red mullet

Side dishes

Arroz	*arrosh*	Rice
Azeitonas	*azayeetoonash*	Olives
Batatas	*batahtash*	Potatoes
Batatas fritas	*batahtash freetash*	Chips
Alho frances	*alyoo fransezh*	Leek
Couve-flor	*kohv-flohr*	Cauliflower
Rabanete	*rabaneht*	Radish
Alface	*alfass*	Lettuce

Desserts

Mousse de chocolate	*mooss d shookoolaht*	Chocolate mousse
Ameixas de elvas	*amayeeshash d elvash*	Preserved greengages
Doces de amêndoa	*dossesh d amengdooa*	Marzipan cakes
Figos com amêndoas	*feegoosh kong amengdooash*	Dried figs studded with almonds
Arroz doce	*arrosh*	Creamy, cold rice pudding
Toucinho do céu	*tohseenyoo do sayoo*	Rich almond and cinnamon cake
Bolo de caco	*boola d kakoo*	Honey cake
Pudim flan	*poodeeng flann*	Crème caramel
Leite creme	*layeet krem*	Caramelised egg custard
Ovos moles	*ohvoosh moolsh*	Egg dessert
Pão de ló	*paowng d loh*	Light sponge cake
Barriga de freiras	*barreega d frayeerash*	Sweet egg-based dessert
Melão	*melaowng*	Melon
Ananás	*ananash*	Pineapple
Cereja	*serehzha*	Cherry
Uvas	*oovash*	Grapes
Toranja	*toorangzha*	Grapefruit
Morango	*moorangoo*	Strawberry
Banana	*bananna*	Banana

Served cold

Arroz doce is a type of rice pudding, but not as the Brits know it. Enriched with eggs and flavoured with lemon zest and cinnamon, it is served cold in small dishes and is, justly, a great favourite.

Drinks

Portuguese	Phonetic	English
Vinho tinto	*veenyoo teengtoo*	Red wine
Vinho branco	*veenyoo brangkoo*	White wine
Vinho verde	*veenyoo vayrd*	Green wine
Cerveja	*serrvezha*	Beer
Cerveja preta	*serrvezha prehta*	Black beer
Imperial	*eengpereeal*	Small draught beer
Caneca	*kanehka*	Large draught beer
Água mineral	*agwa meeneral*	Mineral water
- com gás	*- kong gas*	- sparkling
- sem gás	*- seng gas*	- still
Batido	*bateedoo*	Milk-shake
Bica	*beeka*	Espresso
Café	*kaffeh*	Coffee
Galão	*galaowng*	Tall, milky coffee
Meia de leite	*mayeea d layeet*	Half coffee, half milk
Italiano	*eetaleeahnoo*	Short, stong expresso coffee
Garoto	*garootoo*	Small white coffee
Chá	*sha*	Tea
- com leite	*- kong layeet*	- with milk
- com limão	*- kong leemaowng*	- with lemon
Gelo	*zhehloo*	Ice
Sumo	*soomoo*	Juice
Sumo de laranja	*soomoo d larangzha*	Orange juice
Sumo de maçã	*soomoo d massang*	Apple juice
Sumo de tomate	*soomoo d toomaht*	Tomato juice
Sumo de ananás	*soomoo d ananash*	Pineapple juice
Limonada	*leemonahda*	Lemon juice
Ginginha	*zheengzheenya*	Cherry brandy
Amarguinha	*amargheenya*	Almond liquer
Chocolate quente	*shookoolaht kennt*	Hot chocolate

Snacks

Portuguese	Phonetic	English
Tosta	*tooshta*	Toasted sandwich
Tosta mista	*tooshta meeshta*	Toasted cheese and ham sandwich
Prego no pão	*prehgoo no paowng*	Steak sandwich
Cachorro quente	*kashorroo kennt*	Hot dog
Pizza	*Peetza*	Pizza
Iogurte	*yohgoort*	Yogurt
Pastel de bacalhau	*pashtel d bakalyaow*	Dried cod savoury

Rissol de camarão	*reessol d karnaraowng*	Shrimp rissole
Ovo estrelado	*oovoo ishtralahdoo*	Fried egg
Ovo cozido	*oovoo kozeedoo*	Boiled egg
Ovos mexidos	*oovoosh mesheedoosh*	Scrambled eggs
Ovo escalfado	*oovoo ishkalfahdoo*	Poached egg
Omelete	*omeleht*	Omelette
- de queijo	*- d kayeezhoo*	Cheese omelette
- de fiambre	*- d feeambr*	Ham omelette
- mista	*- meeshta*	Cheese and ham omelette
- de camarão	*- d karnaraowng*	Shrimp omelette
Croquette	*krokett*	Meat savoury
Sandes de...	*sangdesh d...*	...sandwich
- queijo	*- kayeezhoo*	- cheese
- fiambre	*- feeambr*	- Ham
- presunto	*- prezoongtoo*	- smoked ham
- ovo	*- oovoo*	- egg
- carne assada	*- karrn assahda*	- roast meat
- mista	*- meeshta*	- cheese and ham
Bifana	*beefana*	Fried pork roll with mustard

On the thin side

Portuguese steak
(**bife**) is usually a thin
slice of fried beef or
pork served with
chips and black olives.
A **bife com ovo a
cavalo** – literally
'steak with an egg on
horseback' – comes
topped with a fried
egg. Ask for **um bife
grelhado** if you want
your steak grilled.

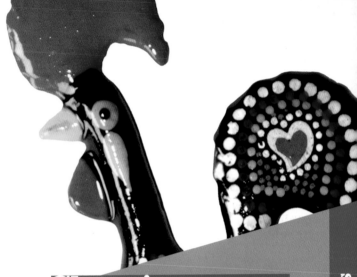

Shopping

The country has taken to supermarkets and giant shopping centres in a big way. But small, traditional shops and markets continue to thrive. Every region offers a wealth of traditional handicrafts, including ceramics, tiles, baskets, embroidery, toys and leather goods. Explore regional traditions through cheeses, sausages, ham, honey, crystallised fruit and wine.

Many consider Porto, at the heart of the country's textile and footwear industries, a better shopping city than Lisbon. But both offer a rich selection, from the bargains of flea markets to the high fashion of exclusive boutiques.

Essentials

Where can I buy...?	Onde posso comprar...?	ongd possoo kong-prar...?
I'd like to buy...	Quero comprar...	kayroo kongprar...
Do you have...?	Tem...?	teng...?
I'd like this	Quero ficar com isto	kayroo feekar kong ishtoo
I'd prefer...	Preferia...	preffereea...
Could you show me...?	Pode mostrar-me...?	pood moshtrar-me...?
I'm just looking, thanks	Estou só a ver, obrigado/a	ishtoou soh a vayr, ohbreegahdoo/a

How much is it?	Quanto custa?	kwangtoo kooshta?
Could you write down the price?	Pode escrever o preço?	pood ishkrevayr o praysoo?
Do you have any items on sale?	Tem artigos em saldo?	teng arteegoosh eng saldoo?
Could I have a discount?	Pode fazer um desconto?	pood fazayr oong deshkongtoo?
Nothing else, thanks	Mais nada, obrigado	mash nahda, ohbreegahdoo
Do you accept credit cards?	Aceite cartões de credito?	assayt kartongsh d kredeetoo?

Could you post it to...?	Pode enviar por correio para...?	pood engveeyar por koorrayoo para...?
Can I exchange it?	Posso trocá-lo?	possoo trossah-lo?
I'd like to return this	Quero devolver isto	kayroo devolvayr ishtoo
I'd like a refund	Quero o reembolso	kayroo o rehem-bolsoo

Local specialities

Every region has something special to offer. The island of Madeira is famous for its fine lace and hand-embroidered tablecloths. Northern Minho is the place to buy filigree jewellery. Cork from the Alentejo creates anything from umbrellas to decorative boxes. Fisherman's shirts and sweaters from Nazaré and other ports are both colourful and warm.

| Can you recommend a shop selling local specialities? | Pode recomendar uma loja que venda especia-lidades locais? | pood rekomengdar oonga lohzha k vengda ispseealee-dahdesh lokaheesh? |

What should I buy from here?	**O que é que devo comprar aqui?**	*o k eh k devoo kongprar akee?*
Is... (leather) good quality?	**(A pele) é de boa qualidade?**	*(a pe-le) eh d boa kwaleedahd?*
Do you make the... (ceramics) yourself?	**É o senhor/a que faz (a cerâmica)?**	*eh o senyoor/a k faz (a serameeka)?*
Is it hand made?	**É feito a mão?**	*eh fayeetoo a maowng?*
Do you make it to measure?	**Fazem à medida?**	*fazeng ah medeeda?*
Can I order one?	**Posso encomendar um/uma?**	*possoo enkomendar oong/oonga?*

Bag a carpet

Arraiolos is famous for colourful carpets hand-stitched by the small town's women. The woollen carpets feature eighteenth-century floral designs and are available all over the Alentejo region.

Popular things to buy

Bordado de Madeira	*bordahdoo d Madayeera*	Embroidery, from Madeira
Brinquedos de madeira	*bringkehdoosh d madayeera*	Handmade wooden toys
Cerâmica	*serameeka*	Pottery
Cestos	*saystoosh*	Handmade baskets
Chouriço	*shohreesoo*	Spicy sausage
Colchas de Castelo Branco	*kolshash d kashteloo brangkoo*	Embroidered bedspreads from Castelo Branco
Filigrana	*feeleegrana*	Filigree jewellery
Mel	*mel*	Honey

Produtos de cortiça	*proo<u>doo</u>tosh d coor<u>tees</u>sa*	Cork products from the Alentejo
Produtos de pele	*proo<u>doo</u>toosh d pel*	Leather belts, bags and shoes
Queijo da serra	*ka<u>yee</u>zhoo da <u>ser</u>ra*	Soft cheese made from ewe's milk
Vinho de Porto	*<u>vee</u>nyoo d <u>pohr</u>too*	Port wine from the Douro Valley
Vinho verde	*<u>vee</u>nyoo vayrd*	Sparkling "green" wine
Xailes	*<u>shy</u>elsh*	Brightly printed shawls

Send a bottle home

Most specialist wine shops are happy to package and ship crates. This not only lightens your luggage, but also ensures against breakages.

Clothes & shoes

The Portuguese like to dress well, but are not particularly adventurous. The favourite style is "smart casual". The country's textile industry produces for the big international brands, but local designers are beginning to market collections. The top spot for cutting-edge boutiques is Lisbon's Bairro Alto district.

Where is the... department?	**Onde fica a secção...**	*ongd <u>fee</u>ka a sek-<u>sa</u>owng...*
- clothes	**- de roupa?**	*- d <u>roo</u>upa?*
- shoe	**- de sapatos?**	*- d sa<u>pa</u>toosh?*
- women's	**- para mulheres?**	*- <u>pa</u>ra mool<u>yay</u>resh?*
- men's	**- para homens?**	*- <u>pa</u>ra <u>oh</u>mengsh?*
- children's	**- para crianças?**	*- <u>pa</u>ra kree<u>angs</u>ash?*

Well-heeled
Portugal is a major producer of footwear. Most shoes are exported, but trendy, young Portuguese designers now are marketing bright, colourful lines.

I'm looking for...	**Estou à procura de...**	*ishtoou ah prookoora d...*
- a skirt	**- uma saia**	*- oonga sahla*
- trousers	**- calças**	*- kalsash*
- a top	**- um top**	*- oong top*
- a jacket	**- um casaco**	*- oong kasakoo*
- a T-shirt	**- uma T-shirt**	*- oonga te-shert*
- jeans	**- um par de jeans**	*- oong par d zheensh*
- shoes	**- sapatos**	*- sapahtoosh*
- underwear	**- roupa interior**	*- rooupa engtereeohr*
Can I try it on?	**Posso experimentar?**	*possoo esh-pereemengtar?*
What size is it?	**Qual é o tamanho?**	*kwal eh o tamanyoo?*
My size is...	**O meu tamanho é...**	*o mayoo tamanyoo eh...*
- small	**- pequeno**	*- pekaynoo*
- medium	**- médio**	*- mehdeeoo*
- large	**- grande**	*- grangd*
- (see clothes size conversion table on p.96 for full range of sizes)		
Do you have this in my size?	**Tem isto no meu tamanho?**	*teng ishtoo no mayoo tamanyoo?*

Shop till you drop

Stores open at 9am and close at 7pm. Smaller outlets may close for lunch from 1pm to 3pm. But Portugal's many shopping centres usually remain open from 10am to 11pm, including Sundays.

Where is the changing room?	**Onde fica o vestuário?**	ongd _fee_ka o vesh-too_ah_reeoo?
It doesn't fit	**Não me serve**	naowng me sayrv
It doesn't suit me	**Não me fica bem**	naowng me _fee_ka beng
Do you have a... size?	**Tem um tamanho...**	teng _oong_ ta_many_oo...
- bigger	**- maior?**	- my_oor_?
- smaller	**- mais pequeno?**	- mash pe_kay_noo?
Do you have it/them in...	**Tem em...**	teng eng...
- black?	**- preto?**	- _pray_too?
- white?	**- branco?**	- _brang_koo?
- blue?	**- azul?**	- a_zool_?
- green?	**- verde?**	- vayrd?
- red?	**- vermelho?**	- ver_may_lyoo?
Are they made of leather?	**São de pele?**	saowng d pel?
I'm going to leave it/them	**Não vou ficar com ele/ela**	naowng voou fee_kar_ kong el/_ehl_a
I'll take it/them	**Vou ficar com ele/ela**	voou fee_kar_ kong el/_ehl_a
Where can I find...	**Onde posso encontrar...**	ongd _poss_oo engkong_trar_...

You may hear...

Posso ajudâ-lo/la?	possoo azhoodah-loo/la?	Can I help you?
Qual tamanho?	kwal tamanyoo?	What size?
Não temos	naowng taymoosh	We don't have any
Aqui tem	akee teng	Here you are
Mais alguma coisa?	mash algooma koyeeza?	Anything else?
Quer que eu embrulhe?	kayr k ayoo eng-broolye?	Shall I wrap it for you?
Custa... (50) euros	kooshta... (seengk-wengta) ayooroos	It's... (50) euros

Where to shop

Where can I find...	Onde posso encontrar...	ongd possoo engkongtrar
- a bookshop?	- uma livraria?	- oonga leevrarreea?
- a clothes shop?	- uma loja de roupa?	- oonga lozha d rooupa?
- a department store?	- uns grandes armazéns?	- oongs grangdesh armazengsh?
- a gift shop?	- uma loja de prendas?	- oonga lozha d prengdash?
- a music shop?	- uma loja de música?	- oonga lozha d moozeeka?
- a market?	- um mercado?	- oong merkadoo?
- a newsagent?	- uma banca de jornais?	- oonga bangka d zhornayeesh?
- a shoe shop?	- uma sapataria?	- oonga sapatareea?
- a tobacconist?	- uma tabacaria?	- oonga tabakareea?
- a souvenir shop	- uma loja de lembranças?	- oonga lozha d lengbrangshash?

Azulejos

Azulejos, which comes from Arabic, is the Portuguese word for those beautiful ceramic tiles. Antique ones are expensive, but historic reproductions are more reasonably priced.

| What's the best place to buy...? | **Qual é o melhor sítio para comprar...?** | *kwal eh o melyoor seeteeo para kongprar...?* |

I'd like to buy...	**Quero comprar...**	*kayroo kongprar...*
- a film	**- um rolo fotográfico**	*- oong rooloo footografeekoo*
- an English newspaper	**- um jornal inglês**	*- oong zhornal eenglaysh*
- a map	**- um mapa**	*- oong mapa*
- postcards	**- postais**	*- pooshtaeesh*
- a present	**- uma prenda**	*- oonga prengda*
- stamps	**- selos**	*- sayloosh*
- sun cream	**- creme solar**	*- krem sohlar*

Food & markets

| Is there a supermarket/ market nearby? | **Há um supermercado/mercado próximo?** | *ah oom soopermairkahdoo/mair kahdoo proseemoo?* |

Can I have...	**Pode dar-me...**	*pood dar-me...*
- some bread?	**- pão?**	*- paowng?*
- some fruit?	**- fruta?**	*- froota?*
- some cheese?	**- queijo?**	*- kayeezhoo?*
- a bottle of water?	**- uma garrafa de água?**	*- oonga garraffa d agwa?*
- a bottle of wine?	**- uma garrafa de vinho?**	*- oonga garraffa d veenyoo?*

Port wine

There is no better to place to learn about, taste and purchase port wine than in the Douro Valley, where the grapes grow, or in Porto, where the fortified wine is aged.

Getting around

Most visitors fly direct to Lisbon, the southern Algarve coast or Porto in the north. Modern road and rail networks make it easy to cross over from Spain, and ocean liners dock regularly. Hundreds of kilometres of new motorways criss-cross the country, making every major town easy to reach by car. Travelling by rail and bus is a cheap and authentically local way of getting around. Additionally, riders don't have to contend with the dangerous tendencies of some Portuguese drivers. Sleek new metro systems, amiable old trams, modern buses and cheap taxis make city navigation simple.

Arrival

Low-cost airlines fly regularly to Lisbon, Faro in the Algarve and Porto. Most taxi drivers are trustworthy, but a few airport sharks trawl for gullible foreigners. Check the average fares on display in arrival lounges or buy pre-paid taxi fares at the airport. For good hire car prices – and better organisation – book ahead.

Where is/are...	**Onde está/estão...**	*ongd eshtah/esh-taowng...*
- the luggage from flight...?	**- a bagagem do voo...?**	*- a bagahzheng doo vohoo...?*
- the lost luggage office?	**- o balcão da bagagem perdida?**	*- o balkaowng da bagahzheng per-rdeeda?*

Where is/are...	**Onde está/estão...**	*ongd eshtah/esh-taowng...*
- the buses?	**- os autocarros?**	*- osh aowtookar-roosh?*
- the trains?	**- os comboios?**	*- osh congboyoosh?*
- the taxis?	**- os táxis?**	*- osh taksish?*
- the car rental?	**- os carros para alugar?**	*- osh karroosh para aloogar?*
- the exit?	**- a saída?**	*- a sayeeda?*
How do I get to Hotel...?	**Como se vai para o Hotel...?**	*kohmoo se vayee para o otell...?*
My baggage...	**A minha bagagem...**	*a meenya bagahzheng...*
- is lost	**- está perdida**	*- eshtah perrdeeda*

Take a tram

Lisbon's distinctive yellow-and-white trams (**eléctricos**) are the perfect way to tour the city. The No. 28 trundles through historic neighbourhoods and offers excellent views of the Tagus river.

- is damaged	- está danificada	- eshtah daneefeekahda
- has been stolen	- foi roubada	- fohee rohbahdoo

Customs

EU citizens pass rapidly through passport checks. Non-EU citizens may face queues at busy periods. All border controls between Spain and Portugal have been abolished. Travellers are subject to occasional spot checks, but a signpost is usually the only indication that you have crossed from one country to another.

The children are on this passport	As crianças estão registadas neste passaporte	ash kreeansash eshtaowng rezheeshtadash nesht passaport
We're here on holiday	Estamos aqui em férias	estamos akee eng fehreeash
I'm going to...	Vou para...	voh para...
I have nothing to declare	Não tenho nada para declarar	naowng teng nada para dehklarar
Do I have to declare this?	Tenho que declarar isto?	teng k declarar ishtoo?

Car hire

Tourism is one of Portugal's biggest industries, so hire cars are readily available at all airports, and in most towns and resorts. Local companies usually charge lower rates than the big international firms, such as Avis and Hertz. Reserve ahead for lower fares – and to ensure the car is ready when you arrive.

I'd like to hire a...	Gostava de alugar um...	gooshtahva d aloogar oong...
- car	- carro	- karro
- people carrier with...	- monovolume com...	- mohnoovooloom cong...
- air conditioning	- ar condicionado	- ar kongdeeseeo-nahdoo
- automatic transmission	- mudanças automáticas	- moodangsash aowtomaticash
How much is that for...	Quanto custa alugar durante...	kwantoo cooshta aloogar doorangt..

- a day?	- um dia?	- _oong deea?_
- a week?	- uma semana?	- _oonga semana?_
Does that include...	Inclui...	_inklooi..._
- mileage?	- os quilómetros?	- _osh keelometroosh?_
- insurance?	- o seguro?	- _o segooroo?_

On the road

Portugal has a high road-accident rate. Caution is a must for drivers, who endure imprudent overtaking and excessive speeding. The signpost system is spotty at best, so purchase a good atlas and be patient. Motorways charge tolls. Free street parking can be sparse in busy cities. Metered spaces and paid lots avoid bother and are not expensive.

What is the speed limit?	Qual é o limite de velocidade?	_kwal eh o leemeet d velooseedahd?_
Can I park here?	Posso estacionar aqui?	_possoo eeshtaseeyonar akee_
Where is a petrol station?	Onde está o posto de gasolina?	_ongd eshtah o poshto d gazooleena?_
Please fill up the tank with...	Por favor, encha o depósito com...	_pohr favohr, engsha o depozeetoo cong..._
- unleaded	- gasolina sem chumbo	- _gazooleena seng shoongboo_
- diesel	- gasóleo	- _gazohleeoo_
- leaded	- gasolina com chumbo	- _gazooleena cong shoongboo_

Directions

Is this the road to...?	Esta é a estrada para...?	_eshta eh a eshtrada para...?_
How do I get to...?	Como vou para...?	_kohmoo voh para...?_
How far is it to...?	Qual é a distância para...?	_kwal eh a dishtanseea para...?_
How long will it take to...?	Quanto tempo leva para chegar a...?	_kwantoo tengpoo lehva para sheggar a...?_
Could you point it out on the map?	Pode indicar no mapa?	_pood indeekar noo mapa?_
I've lost my way	Estou perdido	_eshtoou perrdeedoo_
On the right/left	À direita/esquerda	_ah deerayta/eeshkayrda_
Turn right/left	Vire à direita/esquerda	_veer ah deerayta/eeshkayrda_

Straight ahead	**Sempre em frente**	_sengpre eng frengt_
Turn around	**Volte para trás**	_vohlt para trash_

Public transport

Public transport is plentiful and cheap. Hail a passing taxi (rates increase after 10pm), hop a bus or tram in big towns, or ride in comfort on the Lisbon and Porto metro systems. An excellent train service whisks passengers between these two cities, and to Faro in under three hours. For real economy, travel long-distance on the air-conditioned express buses.

Ferry 'cross the Tagus
Lisbon's commuter ferries double as budget sightseeing tours across the Tagus. The cost is minimal and there are plenty of seafood bars to sample on the south bank

Bus	**Camioneta**	_kamionehta_
Bus station	**Estação de**	_eeshtasaowng d_
	camionetas	_kamionehtash_
Train	**Comboio**	_kongboyoo_
Train station	**Estação de**	_eeshtasaowng d_
	comboios	_kongboyosh_
I would like to go to...	**Quero ir para...**	_kehroo eer para..._
I would like a...	**Quero um**	_kehroo oong_
ticket	**bilhete...**	_beelyayt..._
- single	**- só de ida**	_- soh d eeda_
- return	**- de ida e volta**	_- d eeda e volta_
- first class	**- de primeira**	_- d preemayeera_
	classe	_class_

- smoking/non-smoking	**- de fumador/não fumador**	*- d fooma<u>dohr</u>/ naowng_fooma<u>dohr</u>*
What time does it leave/arrive?	**A que horas parte/chega?**	*a k <u>or</u>ash part/ <u>she</u>gga?*
Could you tell me when to get off?	**Pode dizer-me onde sair?**	*pood dee<u>zair</u>-me ongd sa<u>eer</u>?*

Taxis

I'd like a taxi to...	**Quero um táxi para...**	*<u>keh</u>roo <u>oong</u> <u>tak</u>si <u>pa</u>ra...*
How much is it to the...	**Quanto custa para o...**	*<u>kwan</u>too <u>coosh</u>ta <u>pa</u>ra o...*
- airport?	**- aeroporto?**	*- aehroh<u>pohr</u>too?*
- town centre?	**- centro da cidade?**	*- <u>seen</u>troo da see<u>dahd</u>?*
- hotel?	**- hotel?**	*- o<u>tell</u>?*

Tours

A wide range of tours and excursions is available to visitors in most towns and resorts. Guides almost invariably speak good English. Wildlife, marine and wine-tasting trips – run by specialists – showcase Portugal's natural riches. A guided tour of Benfica's "Stadium of Light" in Lisbon is a must for football fans.

Are there any organised tours of the town/region?	**Há visitas guiadas da cidade/ região?**	*ah vee<u>zee</u>tash ghee<u>ah</u>-dash da see<u>dahd</u>/ rezhee<u>aowng</u>?*
Where do they leave from?	**Donde partem?**	*dongd <u>par</u>teng?*
What time does it start?	**A que horas começa?**	*a k <u>or</u>ash co<u>may</u>sa?*
Do you have English-speaking guides?	**Tem guias que falam inglês?**	*teng <u>ghee</u>ash k <u>fa</u>lang in<u>glesh</u>?*
Is lunch/tea included?	**O almoço/lanche está incluído?**	*o al<u>moh</u>soo/langsh esh<u>ta</u> eenkloo-<u>ee</u>doo?*
Do we get any free time?	**Temos algum tempo livre?**	*<u>teh</u>moosh al<u>goong</u> <u>teng</u>poo <u>lee</u>vre?*
Are we going to see...?	**Vamos ver...?**	*<u>va</u>moosh vayr...?*
What time do we get back?	**A que horas chegamos?**	*a k <u>or</u>ash she<u>ggah</u>-moosh?*

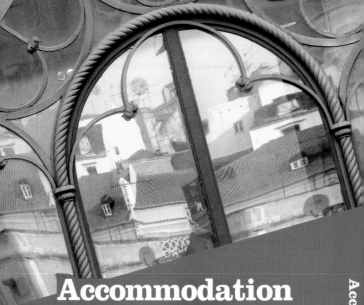

Accommodation

Accommodation in Portugal is as varied as the landscape. Hotels cater for every pocket and taste. Bed-and-breakfasts link into several networks; the best-known is called **Associação de Turismo de Habitação** (www.turihab.pt). The group lists **casas antigas** (elegant manor houses), **quintas e herdades** (agricultural farms and estates) and **casas rústicas** (simple rural homes in a regional style).

Golf is booming; the hotels tend to match the prestige of the courses. For elegance and local colour, try a **pousada** – a heritage building. Just remember that prior booking is essential and prices are high. The **pensão** and the **residencial** provide basic accommodation, but do not always offer the best price – quality ratio. Prices vary considerably between the high season (summer, Easter, Christmas) and the low season.

Types of accommodation

Increasingly, families and friends rent self-catering villas, preferring comfort and immersion to a far-ranging tour. However, those driving through the countryside should seek bed-and-breakfasts in country cottages, manor houses or farms. **Pousadas** and **estalagems** are usually historic, picturesque and pricey.

I'd like to stay in...	**Quero ficar...**	_keh_roo fee_kar_...
- an apartment	**- num apartamento**	- noom aparrta_meen_too
- a campsite	**- num parque de campismo**	- noom _parrk_ d kam_peez_moo
- a hotel	**- num hotel**	- noom o_tell_
- an apart-hotel	**- num aparthotel**	- noom a_parr_totell
- a youth hostel	**- numa estalagem de juventude**	- _noo_ma eeshta-_lah_zheng d zhooven_tood_
- a guest house	**- numa pensão**	- _noo_ma pen_saow_
Is it...	**É...**	eh...
- full board?	**- pensão completa?**	- pen_saow_ kong_pleh_ta?
- half board?	**- meia pensão?**	- _may_a pen_saow_?
- self-catering?	**- com cozinha própria?**	- long koo_zee_nya _pro_preeya?

To the manor born

A special sort of bed-and-breakfast, known as **turismo de habitação**, opens the doors of historic **quintas** (manor houses), villas and country homes. Visit www.turihab.pt or enquire at any Portuguese tourism office.

Reservations

Do you have any rooms available?	**Tem quartos livres?**	*teng kwartoosh leevresh?*
Can you recommend anywhere else?	**Pode recomendar outro sítio?**	*pooday rehcoomendar ohtroo seetioo?*
I'd like to make a reservation for...	**Quero fazer uma reserva para...**	*kehroo fahzayr oonga rehzayrva para...*
- tonight	- **esta noite**	*- ayshta noyt*
- one night	- **uma noite**	*- oonga noyt*
- two nights	- **duas noites**	*- dooash noyeetesh*
- a week	- **uma semana**	*- oonga semana*
From... (May 1st) to... (May 8th)	**De... (dia um de Maio) a... (dia oito de Maio)**	*d... (deeah oong d mahyoo) a... (deeah oheetoo d mahyoo)*

Room types

Almost all rooms, except in basic **pensões**, have a telephone and TV, as well as a mini bar and air conditioning. Ask for the quietest side, if you're worried about noise. Expect to pay extra for the best views. Most hotels happily add extra beds for children or small groups. Many larger establishments offer special business services.

Do you have a... room?	**Tem um quarto...**	*teng oong kwarrtoo...*
- single	- **individual?**	*- indiveedooal?*
- double	- **duplo?**	*- dooploo?*
- family	- **familiar?**	*- fahmeeleear?*
with...	**com...**	*cong...*
- a cot?	- **uma cama de criança?**	*- oonga kahma d kreeangsa?*
- twin beds?	- **camas individuais?**	*- kahmash indiveedooaeesh?*
- a double bed?	- **uma cama de casal?**	*- oonga kahma d kazahl?*
- a bath/shower?	- **uma banheira/ duche?**	*- oonga banyayeera/dooch?*
- air conditioning?	- **ar condicionado?**	*- ar kongdeeseeeonahdoo?*
- internet access?	- **Internet?**	*- eenterrnet?*
Can I see the room?	**Posso ver o quarto?**	*possoo veyr oo kwarrtoo?*

Prices

As might be expected, more stars mean greater luxury – and higher rates. However, what you see is what you get: breakfast and VAT are typically included in the price. The **pensão** and the **residencial** are the cheapest accommodations available, but often lack comfort and charm, especially in big cities. Tipping in hotels is not obligatory, but it's the norm.

How much is...	**Qual é o preço...**	*kwal eh oo praysoo...*
- a double room?	**- dum quarto duplo?**	*- doong kwarrtoo dooploo?*
- per night?	**- por noite?**	*- pohr noyt?*
- per week?	**- por semana?**	*- pohr semana?*
Is breakfast included?	**Inclui o pequeno-almoço?**	*eenklooye oo pehkaynoo-almohsoo?*
Do you have...	**Tem...**	*teng...*
- a reduction for children?	**- um desconto para crianças?**	*- oong deshkongtoo para kreeangsash?*
- a single room supplement?	**- suplemento de quarto individual?**	*- sooplehmengtoo d kwarrtoo indivee-dooal?*
Is there...	**Tem...**	*teng...*
- a swimming pool?	**- piscina?**	*- peeshseena?*
- an elevator?	**- elevador?**	*- elehvadohr?*

Join the inn crowd

Private management has improved Portugal's formerly state-run **pousadas**, or inns. These small, peaceful havens include converted palaces, mansions and convents. But the charm comes at a price – a high one.

I'll take it	Fico com ele	*feekoo cong ehlle*
Can I pay by...	Posso pagar com...	*possoo pagarr kong...*
- credit card?	- um cartão de crédito?	- *oong kartaowng d kredeetoo?*
- traveller's cheques?	- cheques de viagem?	- *shekesh d veeahzheng?*

Special requests

Could you...	Pode...	*poodeh...*
- put this in the hotel safe?	- por isto no cofre do hotel?	- *por ishtoo no cofr doo otell?*
- order a taxi for me?	- chamar um táxi para mim?	- *shamar oong taksi para ming?*
- wake me up at (7am)?	- acordar-me às (sete de manhã)?	- *akorrdar-me ash (sett d manyah)?*

I would like a...	Quero um ...	*kehroo oong...*
- room with a sea view	- quarto com vista para o mar	- *kwarrtoo cong veeshta para oo marr*
- bigger room	- quarto maior	- *kwarrtoo mahyoor*
- quieter room	- quarto mais sossegado	- *kwarrtoo maeesh soosehgahdoo*

Is there...	Tem...	*teng...*
- a safe?	- um cofre?	- *oong cofr?*
- a babysitting service?	- serviço de babysitter?	- *serrveesoo d babysitter?*
- a laundry service?	- serviço de lavandaria?	- *serrveesoo d lavahndareea?*

Is there wheelchair access?	Tem acesso para cadeiras de roda?	*teng asehsoo para kadayeeras d roda?*

Checking in & out

I have a reservation for tonight	Tenho uma reserva para esta noite	*tenyoo oonga rezayrva para ayshta noyt*
In the name of...	No nome de...	*noh nohm d...*
Here's my passport	Aqui está o meu passaporte	*akee ishta oo mayoo passaporrt*
What time is check out?	A que horas é o checkout?	*ah k orash eh oh checkout?*

Can I have a later check out?	**Posso fazer o checkout mais tarde?**	*possoo fahzayr oo checkout maeesh tarrd?*
Can I leave my bags here?	**Posso deixar a minha bagagem aqui?**	*possoo dayeeshar ah meenya bagahzheng akee?*
I'd like to check out	**Quero fazer o checkout**	*kehroo fahzayr oo checkout*
I'd like my bill	**Quero a minha conta**	*kehroo fahzayr ah meenya kongta*

Camping

Do you have...	**Tem...**	*teng...*
- a site available?	**- um lugar livre?**	*- oonga loogar leevr?*
- electricity?	**- electricidade?**	*- eelehtreeseedahd?*
- hot showers?	**- duches quentes?**	*- doochesh kengtesh?*
- tents for hire?	**- tendas para aluguer?**	*- tengdash para aloogair?*

How much is it per...	**Quanto custa por...**	*kwantoo cooshta pour...*
- tent?	**- tenda?**	*- tehnda?*
- caravan?	**- caravana?**	*- karavana?*
- person?	**- pessoa?**	*- pessoha?*
- car?	**- automóvel?**	*- owtomovel?*

Under canvas

The mild weather makes Portugal an ideal country for camping. There are plenty of sites to choose from at reasonable prices, including several close to the big cities. The amenities are often extensive, but usually cost extra.

Survival guide

Portugal has a modern and technologically advanced banking system. The slick **multibanco** network links all cash machines and accepts British cards. Banks do business from 8.30am to 3pm. A few big-city branches open later and on Saturday mornings. However, it's best to avoid cashing traveller's cheques at banks, which charge large commissions. Stick with an exchange (**posto de câmbio**) or euro withdrawals from an ATM (**caixa de multibanco**).

Internet cafés are thin on the ground. Pharmacies are plentiful and identified by a green cross; one in each neighbourhood remains open outside office hours. Facilities for travellers with disabilities are becoming more common, but aren't widespread: ring ahead.

Money & banks

Where is the nearest...	Onde fica... mais próximo?	ongd _feeka... mash prokseemoo?_
- bank?	- o banco	- _o bangkoo_
- ATM/bank machine?	- a caixa de Multibanco	- _a kysha de mooltibangkoo_
- foreign exchange office?	- o posto de câmbio	- _o poshtoo de kangbeeo_
I'd like to...	Quero...	_kayroo..._
- withdraw money	- levantar dinheiro	- _levangtar deenyayroo_
- cash a traveller's cheque	- levantar um cheque de viagem	- _levangtar oong shek d veeyahzheng_
- change money	- trocar dinheiro	- _trohkar deenyayroo_
- arrange a transfer	- fazer uma transferência	- _fazayr oonga trangshferengseea_
What's the exchange rate?	Qual é a taxa de câmbio?	_kwal eh a tasha d kangbeeo?_
What's the commission?	Qual é a comissão?	_kwal eh a komeessaowng?_

Safe & sound

Portugal is relatively safe, but beware of pickpockets, particularly in trams and other crowded places. Sensible precautions should be taken when leaving vehicles unattended.

What's the charge for...	Qual é a taxa para...	_kwal eh a tasha para..._

- making a withdrawal?	**- fazer um levantamento?**	*- fazayr oong leva-mengtoo?*
- cashing a cheque?	**- levantar um cheque?**	*levangtar oong shek?*
This is not right	**Isto não está certo**	*ishtoo naowng esh-tah sehrtoo*
The ATM/bank machine took my card	**O meu cartão ficou retido na caixa de Multibanco**	*o mayoo kartaowng feekoou reteedoo na kysha d mooltibangkoo*
I've forgotten my PIN	**Esqueci-me do meu PIN**	*ishkesee-me doo mayoo peen*

Post office

Where is the (main) post office?	**Onde fica a estação de correios (principal)?**	*ongd feeka a ish-tasaowng d korrayeeoosh (preenseepal)?*
I'd like to send...	**Quero enviar...**	*kayroo engveear...*
- a letter	**- uma carta**	*- oonga karta*
- a postcard	**- um postal**	*- oong poshtal*
- a parcel	**- uma encomenda**	*- oonga engkomengda*
- a fax	**- um fax**	*- oong fax*
I'd like to send this...	**Quero enviar isto...**	*kayroo engveear ishtoo...*
- to the United Kingdom	**- para o Reino Unido**	*- para o rayeenoo ooneedoo*
- by airmail	**- por avião**	*- pohr aveeaowng*
- by express mail	**- por correio expresso**	*- pohr koorrayeeoo eshpressoo*
- by registered mail	**- registada**	*- rezheeshtahda*
I'd like...	**Quero...**	*kayroo...*
- a stamp for this letter/postcard	**- um selo para esta carta/este postal**	*- oong sehloo para ishta karrta/isht poshtal*
- to buy envelopes	**- comprar envelopes**	*- kongprar engvelohpesh*
It's fragile	**É frágil**	*eh frazheel*

51

Telecoms

Where can I make an international phone call?	**Onde posso fazer uma chamada internacional?**	*ongd possoo fazayr oonga shamahda ingtairnasseeonal?*
Where can I buy a phone card?	**Onde posso comprar um cartão telefónico?**	*ongd possoo kongprar oong kartaowng telehfoneekoo?*
How much does it cost per minute?	**Quanto custa por minuto?**	*kwangtoo kooshta por meenootooo?*
The number is...	**O número é...**	*o noomehroo eh...*
What's the area/country code for...?	**Qual é o indicativo nacional/regional de...?**	*kwal eh o eengdeekateevoo nassional/rezhional d...?*
The number is engaged	**O número está impedido**	*o noomehroo ishtah ingpedeedoo*
The connection is bad	**A ligação está mal**	*a leegasaowng ishtah mal*
I've been cut off	**A chamada caiu**	*a shamahda ky-oo*
I'd like a/an...	**Quero um...**	*kayroo oong...*
- charger for my mobile phone	- **carregador para o meu telemóvel**	- *karregadohr para mayoo telemohvel*
- adaptor plug	- **adaptador**	- *adaptadohr*
- pre-paid SIM card	- **cartão SIM pré-pago**	- *kartaowng seeng preh-pahgoo*

Phone boxes

Phone or credit cards are the best option when calling abroad from a phone box. Inside Portugal there are no area codes. Just dial the number, which begins with a "2".

Internet

Where's the nearest Internet café?	**Onde fica o Internet café mais próximo?**	*ongd feeka o eengternet kaffeh mash prokseemoo?*
I'd like to...	**Quero...**	*kayroo...*
- use the Internet	**- utilizar a Internet**	*- ooteeleezar a eengternet*
- check my email	**- ver o meu e-mail**	*- vayr o mayoo e-mehl*
How much is it...	**Quanto custa...**	*kwangtoo kooshta...*
- per minute?	**- por minuto?**	*- por meenootoo?*
- per hour?	**- por hora?**	*- por ohra?*
- to buy a CD?	**- um CD?**	*- oong say-day?*
How do I...	**Como...**	*koomoo...*
- log on?	**- faço o log-on?**	*- fassoo o log-on?*
- open a browser?	**- abro o browser?**	*- abroo o browser?*
- print this?	**- posso imprimir isto?**	*- possoo eengpreemeer ishtoo?*
I need help with this computer	**Preciso de ajuda com este computador**	*presseezoo d azhooda cong isht kongpootadohr*
The computer has crashed	**O computador foi-se abaixo**	*o kongpootadohr foy-s abyshoo*
I've finished	**Acabei**	*Akabay*

Chemist

Where's the nearest (all-night) pharmacy?	**Onde fica a farmácia (em serviço) mais próxima?**	*ongd feeka a farmahseea (eng serrveessoo) mash prokseema?*
I need something for...	**Preciso um medicamento para...**	*presseezoo oom medeekamengtoo para...*
- diarrhoea	**- a diarreia**	*- a deearreea*
- a cold	**- a constipação**	*- a kongshteepasaowng*
- a cough	**- a tosse**	*- a toss*
- insect bites	**- picadas de mosquitos**	*- peekahdash d mooshkeetoosh*

- sunburn	- queimaduras solares	- kaymadoorash solaresh
- motion sickness	- o enjoo	- o engzho-o
- hay fever	- a febre de fenos	- a fehbre d fehnoosh
- period pain	- dores menstruais	- dohresh meng-shtrooaeesh
- abdominal pains	- dores abdominais	- dohresh abdomeenaeesh
- a urine infection	- uma infecção urinária	- oonga ingfeksaowng ooreenahreea

I'd like...	Quero...	kayroo...
- aspirin	- aspirinas	- ashpeereenash
- plasters	- pensos	- pengsoosh
- condoms	- preservativos	- preserrvateevoosh
- insect repellent	- repelente de insectos	- repellengt d insektoosh
- painkillers	- analgésicos	- analzhehzeekoosh
- a contraceptive	- contraceptivos	- kongtrasepteevoosh

How much should I take?	Quanto devo tomar?	kwangtoo dehvoo toomar?
Take...	Tome...	toome...
- a tablet	- um comprimido	- oong kongpreemeedoo
- a teaspoon	- uma colher de chá	- oonga kolyair d shah
- with water	- com água	- kong agwa

How often should I take this?	Quantas vezes devo tomar isto?	kwangtash vayzesh dehvoo toomar ishtoo?
- once/twice a day	- uma vez/duas vezes por dia	- ooma vayz/dooash vayzes por deea
- before/after meals	- antes/depois das refeições	- angtesh/depoysh dash refayeesongsh
- in the morning/ evening	- de manhã/à noite	- d mangya/ah noyt

| Is it suitable for children? | É recomendado a crianças? | eh rekomengdahdoo a kreeangsash? |
| Will it make me drowsy? | Provoca sonolência? | proovooka soonoolengseea? |

English	Portuguese	Pronunciation
Do I need a prescription?	**É necessário receita médica?**	*eh nessessahreeoo resayeeta mehdeeka?*

Children

Where should I take the children?	**Onde posso levar as crianças?**	*ongd possoo lehvar ash kreeangsash?*
Where is the nearest...	**Onde fica... mais próximo/a?**	*ongd feeka... mash prokseemoo/a?*
- playground?	**- o parque infantil**	*- o parrke infangteel*
- fairground?	**- a feira popular**	*- fayra poopoolar*
- zoo?	**- o jardim zoológico**	*- o zhardeeng zo-olo-hzheekoo*
- swimming pool?	**- a piscina**	*- a peeshseena*
- park?	**- o parque**	*- o parrke*
Is this suitable for children?	**É recomendado a crianças?**	*eh rekomengdahdoo a kreeangsash?*
Are children allowed?	**As crianças podem entrar?**	*ash kreeangsash poodeng engtrar?*
Are there baby-changing facilities here?	**Tem fraldário?**	*teng fraldahreeo?*
Do you have a...	**Tem uma...**	*teng oonga...*
- children's menu?	**- ementa para crianças?**	*- emengta para kreeangsash?*
- high chair?	**- cadeira para crianças?**	*- kreeadayeera para kreeangsash?*
Is there a...	**Há um...**	*ah oong...*
- child-minding service?	**- serviço de supervisionamento de crianças?**	*- serrveesseeoo d sooperveezeeeona-mengtoo d kreeangsash?*
- nursery?	**- jardim infantil?**	*- zharrdeeng eeng-fangteel?*
Can you recommend a reliable babysitter?	**Pode-me recomendar um babysitter de confiança?**	*pood-me rekomengdar oom babysitter d kongfeeangsa?*
He/she is... years old	**Ele/ela tem... anos**	*ehl/ela teng... annosh*
I'd like to buy...	**Quero comprar...**	*kayroo kongprar...*

- nappies	- **fraldas**	- _fral_dash
- baby wipes	- **toalhitas de bebé**	- _toalyee_tash d behbeh
- tissues	- **lenços de papel**	- _leng_soosh d pap_pel_

Travellers with disabilities

I have a disability	**Tenho uma deficiência**	_tenyoo oonga defeesyengseea_
I need assistance	**Preciso de ajuda**	_pre_seezoo d a_zhoo_da
I am blind	**Sou cego/a**	_so_-ou _seh_goo/a
I am deaf	**Sou surdo/a**	_so_-ou _soor_dho/a
I have a hearing aid	**Uso um aparelho auditivo**	_oo_zo _oong_ apa_rel_yoo owdee_tee_voo
I can't walk well	**Não sou capaz de andar bem**	naowng _so_-ou ka_paz_ d ang_dar_ beng
Is there a lift?	**Tem elevador?**	teng eleva_dohr_?
Is there wheelchair access?	**Tem acesso para cadeiras de roda?**	teng a_ses_soo _para_ ka_day_eerash d _roh_da?
Can I bring my guide dog?	**Posso trazer o meu cão de guia?**	_pos_soo tra_zayr_ o _may_oo kaowng d _ghee_a?
Are there disabled toilets?	**Tem casas de banho para deficientes?**	teng _ka_zash d _bang_-oo _para_ defeesyeng_tesh_?
Could you help me...	**Pode ajudar-me...**	pood azhoo_dar_-me...
- cross the street?	**- a atravessar a rua?**	- a atraves_sar_ a _roo_a?
- go up/down the stairs?	**- a subir/descer as escadas?**	- a soo_beer_/desh_sayr_ ash ish_kah_das?
Could you call a disabled taxi for me?	**Pode chamar um táxi para deficientes, por favor?**	pood sha_mar_ _oong_ _tak_see para defeesyeng_tesh_, pohr fa_vohr_?

Repairs & cleaning

This is broken	**Isto está avariado/a**	_ish_too ish_tah_ ava-ree_ah_doo/a
Can you fix it?	**Pode arranjar?**	pood arrang_zhar_?
Do you have...	**Tem...**	teng...
- a battery?	**- uma pilha?**	- _oong_a _peel_ya?

- spare parts?	- peças suplentes?	- _pesash sooplengtesh?_

Can you... this?	Pode... isto?	_pood... ishtoo?_
- clean	- limpar	- _leengpar_
- press	- passar	- _passar_
- dry-clean	- limpar a seco	- _leengpar a sehkoo_
- patch	- remendar	- _remendar_
When will it be ready?	Quando fica pronto/a?	_kwangdoo feeka prongtoo/a?_
This isn't mine	Isto não é meu	_ishtoo naowng eh mayoo_

Tourist information

Where's the Tourist Information Office?	Onde fica o posto de turismo?	_ongd feeka o poshtoo d tooreezhmoo?_
Do you have a city/regional map?	Tem um mapa da cidade/região?	_teng oong mapa da seedahd/ rezhaowng?_
What are the main places of interest?	Quais são os principais lugares de interesse?	_kyeesh saowng osh preengseepyeesh loogaresh d ingteress?_
Could you show me on the map?	Pode mostrar-me no mapa?	_pood mooshtrar-me no mapa?_
We'll be here for...	Ficamos aqui...	_feekamoosh akee..._
- half a day	- meio dia	- _mayoo deea_
- a day	- um dia	- _oong deea_
- a week	- uma semana	- _oonga semana_
Do you have a brochure in English?	Tem uma brochura em inglês?	_teng oonga brooshoora eng eenglaysh?_
We're interested in...	Estamos interessados em...	_ishtamosh interssadoosh eng..._
- history	- história	- _ishtohria_
- architecture	- arquitectura	- _arrkeetektoora_
- shopping	- fazer compras	- _fazayr kongprash_
- hiking	- andar a pé	- _angdar a peh_

57

- a scenic walk	- **um passeio a pé para ver a paisagem**	- _oong_ pas_say_oo a peh _para_ vayr a pysa_zheng_
- a boat cruise	- **um passeio de barco**	- _oong_ pas_say_oo d _barr_koo
- a guided tour	- **uma visita guiada**	- _oonga_ vee_zee_ta ghee_ahda_
How long does it take?	**Quanto tempo leva?**	_kwang_too _temp_oo _leh_va?
Are there any tours in English?	**Fazem algumas visitas em inglês?**	_fazheng_ al_goo_mash vee_zee_tash eng een_glay_sh?

Metroland

The metro is the quickest and cheapest way to get around Lisbon and Porto. Buy a ticket before travelling and click it at the barrier when entering and leaving.

Emergencies

Portugal has a relatively low crime rate, but travellers should take sensible precautions. Avoid dark and deserted areas, including parks, at night. Don't leave valuables unattended in cars or at the beach. Pickpockets operate in crowded areas, particularly in trams, markets and metro trains. They sometimes cause a fuss to divert attention, while an accomplice harvests wallets.

EU residents are entitled to free medical care. However, the European Health Insurance Card (EHIC) only covers emergency medical treatment – and private hospitals won't accept it. Thus the UK Foreign Office recommends getting travel and medical insurance.

Medical

Where is the...	Onde fica o...	*ohnd feeka oh...*
- hospital?	- hospital?	*- ohshpital?*
- health centre?	- centro da saúde?	*- sentroo dah saood?*

I need...	Preciso de...	*prehseezoo d...*
- a doctor	- um médico	*- oong mehdeekoo*
- a female doctor	- uma médica do sexo feminino	*- oonga mehdeekoo doo seksoo femineenoo*
- an ambulance	- uma ambulância	*- oonga angboolangseea*

| It's very urgent | É muito urgente | *eh mweengtoo oorzhengt* |
| I'm injured | Estou ferido | *ishtoou fereedoo* |

I have...	Tenho...	*teengyoo...*
- a cold	- uma constipação	*- oonga congshteepasaowng*
- diarrhoea	- diarreia	*- deeareeya*
- a rash	- uma erupção cutânea	*- oonga eroopsaowng cootahnea*
- a temperature	- febre	*- febre*
I have a lump here	Tenho um alto aqui	*teengyoo oong altoo akee*
Can I have the morning-after pill?	Posso ter uma pílula do dia seguinte?	*possoo tehr oonga peeloola doo deeya segheengt?*

| It hurts here | Dói aqui | *doy akee* |
| It hurts a lot/a little | Dói muito/um pouco | *doy mweetoo/oom pohcoo* |

| How much do I owe you? | Quanto devo? | *kwangtoo dehvoo?* |
| I have insurance | Tenho seguro | *teengyoo segooroo* |

Dentist

| I need a dentist | Preciso de um dentista | *prehseezoo d oong dehngteeshta* |
| I have toothache | Tenho uma dor de dentes | *teengyoo oonga dohr d dehngtsh* |

My gums are swollen	**As minhas gengivas estão inchadas**	*ash meengyash zhen-zheevash eshtaowng eenchadash*
This filling has fallen out	**A massa deste dente caiu**	*a massa desht dengt cayoo*
I have an abscess	**Tenho um abcesso**	*teengyoo oong abseessoo*
I've broken a tooth	**Parti um dente**	*partee oong dengt*
Are you going to take it out?	**Vai extraí-lo?**	*vaee eshtraee-l?*

Emergency numbers

For help, dial 112 and specify **polícia**, **ambulância** or **bombeiros** (fire brigade). Accidents and assaults should be officially reported to the police.

Crime

I want to report a theft	**Quero participar um roubo**	*keeroo parteeseepar oong rohboo*
Someone has stolen...	**Alguém roubou...**	*algheng rohboh...*
- my bag	**- a minha mala**	*- a meengya mahla*
- my car	**- o meu carro**	*- o mayoo karroo*
- my credit cards	**- os meus cartões de crédito**	*- osh meyoosh kartaowngsh d kredeetoo*
- my money	**- o meu dinheiro**	*- o mayoo deenyayeeroo*
- my passport	**- o meu passaporte**	*- o mayoo passaport*
I've been attacked	**Fui atacado/a**	*fooee atakahdoo/a*

Lost property

| I've lost... | **Perdi...** | *perrdee...* |
| - my car keys | **- as chaves do carro** | *- ash shahvesh doo karroo* |

- my driving licence	- a minha carta de condução	- a _meeng_ya _carr_ta d kongdoo_saoow_
- my handbag	- a minha mala	- a _meeng_ya _mah_la
- my flight tickets	- os meus bilhetes de avião	- oosh _may_oosh beel_yay_tesh d avee_ya_oowng
I left it in the taxi	Deixei no táxi	dayee_shay_ee noo _tak_si

Breakdowns

I've had...	Tive...	teev...
- an accident	- um acidente	- _oong_ asee_deng_t
- a breakdown	- uma avaria	- _oong_a ava_ree_a
- a puncture	- um furo	- _oong foo_roo
My battery is flat	Estou sem bateria	ish_too_u seng bat_te_ree_a
I don't have a spare tyre	Não tenho um pneu sobresselente	naowng _teng_yoo _oong_ _pnay_oo soobrese_lent_
I've run out of petrol	Não tenho gasolina	naowng _teeng_yoo gazoo_lee_na
My car doesn't start	O meu carro não arranca	o _may_oo _karr_oo naowng ar_rang_ka
Can you repair it?	Pode arranjá-lo?	pood arran_zhar_-l?
I have breakdown cover	Tenho seguro de assistência em viagem	_teeng_yoo se_goo_roo d asseesh_teng_seeya eng vee_yahz_heng

Problems with the authorities

I'm sorry, I didn't realise...	Desculpe, não sabia que...	desh_koolp_, naowng sa_bee_ya k...
- I was driving so fast	- estava a guiar com tanta velocidade	- esh_tah_va a ghee_yar_ kong _tang_ta veloseedahd
- I went over the red lights	- passei a semáforo vermelho	- pas_say_ee a se_maf_oroo ver-rmaylyoo
- it was against the law	- era proibido	- _eh_ra proee_bee_doo
Here are my documents	Aqui estão os meus documentos	_akee_ esh_taowng_ osh dookoo_meng_toosh
I'm innocent	Estou inocente	ish_too_u eenoh_sent_

Dictionary

The English-Portuguese dictionary in this chapter will help you build your own sentences, and the subsequent Portuguese-English one will probably come in handy to decipher the reply. In the Portuguese, we list nouns with their article: **o** for masculine, **a** for feminine and **os/as** for plural. If nouns can be either masculine or feminine, we display both: **amigo/a**, **o/a** (friend) means **o amigo** is a male friend, **a amiga** the female version. For more tips on grammar and pronunciation, see the Introduction.

English-Portuguese dictionary

A

a(n)	um/uma	oong/oonga
about (concerning)	sobre	sobr
accident	acidente, o	aseedengt
accommodation	alojamento, o	aloozhamentoo
A&E	Urgências	oorzhengseeyash
aeroplane	avião, o	aveeaowng, o
after	depois	depoysh
again	outra vez	ooutra vaysh
ago	há	ah
AIDS	SIDA, a	seeda, a
airmail	por avião	pour aviaowng
airport	aeroporto, o	aehrooportoo, o
alarm	alarme, o	alahrrm, o
all	tudo	toodoo
allergy	alergia, a	alairzheea, a
all right	tudo bem	toodoo beng
ambulance	ambulância, a	angboolangshia, a
America	América	ameyreeka
American	Americano/a	ameyreekahnoo/a
and	e	e
another	outro/a	ooutroo/a
to answer	responder	reshpondair
any	qualquer	kwalkair
apartment	apartamento, o	apartamengtoo
appointment	marcação, a	markasaowng, a
April	Abril	abreel
area	área, a	ahreea, a

area code	indicativo	eengdeekateevoo

Portugal no longer has area codes. Inside the country, just dial the number, which begins with a 2. From abroad, add 00 351 to the beginning.

around	perto de	pairtoo d
to arrange	combinar	kongbeenar
arrival	chegada	shegahda
art	arte	arrt
to ask	perguntar	pairgoongtar
aspirin	aspirina, a	aspeereena, a
at	em	eng
at home	em casa	eng kahza
at last	finalmente	feenalmengt
at least	pelo menos	payloo maynoosz
at once	imediatamente	eemaydeeatamengt
attention	atenção	atensaowng
August	Agosto	agoshtoo
Australia	Austrália	aooshtrahleea
Australian	Australiano/a	aooshtrahleeahnoo/a

B

baby	bebé, o	behbeh, o

back (place)	**traseiras**	*trazayeerash*
baggage	**bagagem, a**	*bahgahzheng, a*
bar (pub)	**bar, o**	*bahr, o*
bath	**banheira, a**	*banyayeera, a*
to be	**ser/estar**	*sehr/ishtar*
beach	**praia, a**	*prahyeea, a*
because	**porque**	*porrke*
before	**antes**	*antesh*
best	**melhor, o/a**	*melyor, o/a*
better	**melhor que**	*melyor k*
between	**entre**	*entr*
bicycle	**bicicleta, a**	*beeseekleta, a*
big	**grande**	*grangd*
bill	**conta, a**	*kongta, a*
bit (a)	**bocado, um**	*bookahdoo, oong*
book	**livro, o**	*leevroo, o*
to book	**reservar**	*rezerrvar*
booking	**reserva, a**	*rezerrva, a*
box office	**bilheteira, a**	*beelyetayeera, a*
boy	**rapaz, o**	*rapash, o*
brother	**irmão, o**	*eermaowng, o*
bureau de change	**agência de câmbio, a**	*azhengseea d kam-beeoo, a*
to burn	**queimar**	*kayeemar*
bus	**autocarro, o**	*aowtookarro, o*
business	**negócios**	*negoseeoosh*
business class	**primeira classe**	*preemayra klass*
but	**mas**	*mash*
to buy	**comprar**	*koomprar*
by (via)	**de**	*d*
by (beside)	**ao lado de**	*aow lahdoo d*
by (by air, car, etc)	**de (de avião, carro, etc)**	*d (d aveeaowng, carroo, etc.)*

C

| cab | **táxi, o** | *taksee, o* |

Portuguese taxis are beige or black and green. Hail them or queue at a taxi rank.

café	**café, o**	*kaffeh, o*
to call	**chamar**	*shamar*
camera	**máquina fotográfica, a**	*makeena fotografeeka, a*
can (to be able)	**poder**	*poodayr*
to cancel	**cancelar**	*kanselar*
car	**carro, o**	*karroo, o*
cash	**em dinheiro**	*eng deenyayeeroo*
cash point	**caixa de Multibanco, a**	*kysha d mooltee-bangkoo, a*
cd	**CD, o**	*se de. o*
centre	**centro, o**	*sentroo, o*
to change	**mudar**	*moodar*
charge	**custo**	*kooshtoo*
to charge	**cobrar**	*koobrar*
cheap	**barato**	*barahtoo*
to check in	**fazer o checkin**	*fazayr o shekin*

cheque	**cheque, o**	*sheke, o*
child	**criança, a**	*kreeangsa, a*
church	**igreja, a**	*eegrayzha, a*
cigar	**charuto, o**	*sharooto, o*
cigarette	**cigarro, o**	*seegarroo, o*

| cinema | **cinema, o** | *seenayma, o* |

Films appear in their original language with subtitles.
The Portuguese only dub cartoons.

city	**cidade, a**	*seedahd, a*
to close	**fechar**	*feshar*
close by	**perto de**	*pairtoo d*
closed	**fechado/a**	*feshadoo/a*
clothes	**roupa, a**	*rooupa, a*
club	**clube, o**	*kloob, o*
coast	**costa, a**	*koshta, a*
cold	**frio**	*freeoo*
colour	**cor, a**	*kohr, a*
to come	**vir**	*veer*
to complain	**queixar-se**	*kayshar-se*
complaint	**queixa, a**	*kaysha, a*
to confirm	**confirmar**	*kongfeermar*
confirmation	**confirmação, a**	*kongfeermasaowng*
congratulations!	**parabéns!**	*parabens*
consulate	**consulado, o**	*konsoolahdoo, o*
to contact	**contactar**	*kontaktar*
contagious	**contagioso**	*kongtazheeozoo*
cool	**fresco**	*frayshkoo*
cost	**custo, o**	*kooshtoo, o*
to cost	**custar**	*kooshtar*
country	**país, o**	*paeesh, o*
countryside	**campo, o**	*kampoo, o*
credit card	**cartão de crédito, o**	*kartaowng de kredeet, o*
crime	**crime, o**	*kreem, o*
currency	**moeda, a**	*mooehda, a*
customs	**alfândega, a**	*alfangdega, a*
cut	**corte, o**	*korrt, o*
to cut	**cortar**	*korrtar*

D

date (calendar)	**data, a**	*dahta, a*
daughter	**filha, a**	*feelya, a*
day	**dia, o**	*deea, o*
December	**Dezembro**	*dezhengbroo*
to dehydrate	**desidratar**	*dezeedratar*
delay	**atraso**	*atrassoo*
to dial	**marcar**	*marrkar*
difficult	**difícil**	*deefeesseel*
directions	**direcções**	*deereksongsh*
dirty	**sujo/a**	*soozhoo/a*
disabled	**deficiente**	*defeeseeyengt*
disco	**discoteca, a**	*deeskotehka, a*
discount	**desconto, o**	*deshkongtoo, o*

disinfectant	**desinfectante, o**	*dezeenfektangt, o*
to disturb	**perturbar**	*perrtoorbar*
doctor	**médico, o**	*mehdeekoo, o*
double (room, bed)	**de casal**	*d kazal*
down	**por baixo**	*poor byshoo*
to drive	**conduzir**	*kongdoozeer*
driver	**motorista, o**	*motoreesta, o*
drug	**droga, a**	*drohga, a*
dry-cleaner's	**lavandaria, a**	*lavandareea, a*
during	**durante**	*doorant*
duty (tax)	**taxa, a**	*tasha, a*

E

early	**cedo**	*saydoo*
to eat	**comer**	*comayr*
e-mail	**e-mail, o**	*emmayl, o*
embassy	**embaixada, a**	*engbaeeshahda, a*
emergency	**emergência, a**	*emerrzhengseea, a*
England	**Inglaterra**	*eenglaterra*
English	**Inglês/esa**	*eenglesh/ingleza*
enough	**suficiente**	*soofeeseeyengt*
error	**erro, o**	*erroo, o*
exactly	**precisamente**	*preseezamengt*
exchange rate	**taxa de câmbio, a**	*tasha d kambeeoo, a*
exhibition	**exposição, a**	*ishpoozeesaowng, a*
to export	**exportar**	*ishpoortar*
express (delivery)	**expresso**	*ishpressoo*

| **express (train)** | **expresso, o** | *ishpressoo, o* |

An express train, the Alfa, travels between Lisbon and Porto in just under three hours.

F

facilities	**instalações, as**	*eengshtalasoesh, ash*
far	**longe**	*longzh*
fast	**rápido**	*rapeedoo*
father	**pai, o**	*py, o*
favourite	**preferido/a**	*prefereedoo/a*
to fax	**enviar um fax**	*engveear oom fax*
February	**Fevereiro**	*feverayeeroo*
filling (station)	**abastecimento**	*abasheseemengtoo*
film (camera)	**rolo fotográfico, o**	*rooloo fotografeekoo, o*
film (cinema)	**filme, o**	*feelm, o*
to finish	**acabar**	*akabar*
fire	**fogo, o**	*foogoo, o*
first aid	**primeiros socorros**	*preemayeeroosh sookoorroosh*
fitting room	**provadores**	*proovadorrsh*
flight	**voo, o**	*vo-oo, o*
food poisoning	**intoxicação alimentar, a**	*eengtoxikasaowng aleemengtar, a*
football	**futebol, o**	*footebol, o*
for	**para**	*para*

form (document)	**formulário, o**	*formoolahreeoo, o*
free (vacant)	**livre**	*leevr*
free (money)	**grátis**	*grahtees*
friend	**amigo/a, o/a**	*ameegoo/a, o/a*
from	**de**	*d*

G

gallery	**galeria, a**	*galereea, a*
garage	**garagem, a**	*garahzheng, a*
gas	**gás, o**	*gass, o*
gents	**homens**	*ohmengs*
to get	**arranjar**	*arrangzhar*
girl	**rapariga, a**	*rapareega, a*
to give	**dar**	*dahr*
glasses	**óculos, os**	*okkoolosh, osh*
to go	**ir**	*eer*
golf	**golfe, o**	*golf, o*
good	**bom/boa**	*bong/boa*
group	**grupo, o**	*groopoo, o*
guarantee	**garantia, a**	*garangteea, a*
guide	**guia, o**	*gheea, a*

H

hair	**cabelo, o**	*kabelloo, o*
half	**meio/a**	*meeyoo/a*
to have	**ter**	*tayr*
heat	**calor, o**	*kalohr, o*
help!	**socorro!**	*sokorroo!*
to help	**ajudar**	*azhoodar*
here	**aqui**	*akee*
high	**alto/a**	*altoo/a*
to hire	**alugar**	*aloogar*

holiday	**feriado, o**	*ferreeahdoo, o*

Portugal has 11 national bank holidays a year, including
April 25 (Revolution Day), June 10 (Camões Day) and
October 5 (Republic Day).

holidays	**férias, as**	*faireeash, ash*
homosexual	**homosexual, o**	*omoseksooal, o*
hospital	**hospital, o**	*ospeetal, o*
hot	**quente**	*kennt*
how?	**como?**	*koomoo?*
how big?	**de que tamanho?**	*d k tamanyoo*
how far?	**é muito longe?**	*eh mweetoo longzhe?*
how long?	**durante quanto tempo?**	*doorangt kwangtoo tengpoo?*
how much?	**quanto?**	*kwangtoo?*
to be hungry	**ter fome**	*tayr fom*
hurry up!	**depressa!**	*depressa!*
husband	**marido, o**	*mareedoo, o*

I

identity card	**bilhete de identidade, o**	*beelyet d eedengti-dahd, o*

ill	**doente**	*dooengt*
immediately	**já**	*zha*
to import	**importar**	*eemportar*
important	**importante**	*eemportangt*
in	**em**	*eng*
information	**informação, a**	*eenformasaowng, a*
inside	**dentro**	*dengtroo*
insurance	**seguro, o**	*segooroo, o*
interesting	**interessante**	*interressangt*
international	**internacional**	*interrnaseeonal*
Ireland	**Irlanda**	*eerlangda*
Irish	**Irlandês/esa**	*eerlangdaysh/dayza*
island	**ilha, a**	*eelya, a*
itinerary	**itinerário, o**	*eeteenerahreeoo, o*

J

January	**Janeiro**	*zhanayeeroo*
jellyfish	**alforeca, a**	*alforehka, a*
jet ski	**jet-ski, o**	*zhet-skee, o*
journey	**viagem, a**	*veeahzheng, a*
July	**Julho**	*zhoolyoo*
junction	**entroncamento, o**	*engtroncamengtoo, o*
June	**Junho**	*zhoonyoo*
just (only)	**só**	*soh*

K

to keep	**guardar**	*gwarrdar*
key	**chave, a**	*shav, a*
kid (meat)	**cabrito, o**	*kabreetoo, o*
to kill	**matar**	*mattar*
kind (nice)	**simpático/a**	*seengpatteekoo/a*
kind (sort)	**tipo, o**	*teepoo, o*
kiosk	**quiosque, o**	*keeoshk, o*
kiss	**beijo, o**	*bayeezhoo, o*
to kiss	**beijar**	*bayeezhar*
to know (knowledge)	**saber**	*sabayr*
to know (person)	**conhecer**	*koonyesayr*

L

ladies (toilets)	**senhoras**	*senyoorash*
lady	**senhora, a**	*senyoor, a*
language	**língua, a**	*leengwa, a*
last	**último/a**	*toolteemoo/a*
late (delayed)	**atrasado/a**	*atrassahdoo/a*
late (time)	**tarde**	*tarrd*

| **launderette** | **lavandaria, a** | *lavandareea, a* |

Self-service laundrettes are rare in Portugal. But most dry cleaners also wash laundry.

lawyer	**advogado/a, o/a**	*advoogahdoo/a, o/a*
left	**esquerdo/a**	*eshkehrdoo/a*
less	**menos**	*menoosh*
letter	**carta, a**	*karrta, a*
library	**biblioteca, a**	*beebliooteka, a*

life jacket	colete de salvação, o	kolette d salvasaowng, o
lifeguard	salvavidas, o	salvaveedash, o
to like	gostar	gooshtar
to listen to	escutar	eshkootar
little (a little)	pouco/a	pohkoo/a
local	local	lookal
to look	olhar	ohlyar
to lose	perder	pairdayr
lost property	objectos perdidos, os	obzhetoosh perdee-doosh
luggage	bagagem, a	bagazheng, a

M

madam	minha senhora	meenya senyoora
mail	correio, o	koorayoo, o
main	principal	preenseepal
to make	fazer	fazhayr
man	homem, o	ohmeng, o
manager	gerente, o	zherengt, o
many	muitos	mweetoosh
map (city)	mapa da cidade, o	mapa da seedahd, o
map (road)	mapa das estradas, o	mapa dash eshtrahdash
March	Março	marrsoo
market	mercado, o	maircahdoo, o
married	casado/a	cazahdoo/a
material (cloth)	tecido, o	tesseedoo, o
May	Maio	mahyoo
maybe	talvez	talvesh
meeting	reunião, a	rayooniaowng, a
message	mensagem, a	mengsahzheng, a
midday	meio-dia	meeyoo-deea
midnight	meia-noite	meeya-noyt
minimum	mínimo, o	meeneenoo, o
minute	minuto, o	meenootoo, o
to miss	perder	pairdayr
missing	desaparecido/a	dezapareseedoo/a
mobile phone	telemóvel, o	telemohvel, o
moment	momento, o	moomentoo, o
money	dinheiro, o	deenyayeeroo, o
more	mais	mash
mosquito	mosquito, o	mooshkeetoo, o
most	maioria, a	mayooreea, a
mother	mãe, a	myng, a
much	muito	mweetoo

| museum | museu, o | moozayoo, o |

Museums close on Mondays, but otherwise are open from 10am to 5pm typically.

| must | deve | dehv |
| my | meu/minha | mayoo/meenya |

N

| name | nome, o | nohm, o |

nationality	nacionalidade, a	nasseeonaleedahd, a
near	perto	pairtoo
necessary	necessário	nessesahrioo
to need	precisar	presseezar
never	nunca	noongka
new	novo	noovoo
news	notícias, as	nooteesheeash, ash
newspaper	jornal, o	zhornal, o
next	seguinte	segeengt
next to	perto de	pairtoo d
nice (people)	simpático/a	seengpatteekoo/a
nice (things)	bom/boa	bong/boa
night	noite, a	noyt, a
nightclub	discoteca, a	deeshkoteka, a
north	norte, o	nort, o
note (money)	nota, a	nota, a
nothing	nada	nahda
November	Novembro	noovembroo
now	agora	agohra
nowhere	em lado nenhum	eng lahdoo nenyoong
nudist beach	praia de nudistas, a	prya d noodeeshtash
number	número, o	noomehroo, o

O

object	objecto, o	obzhetoo, o
October	Outubro	oooutoobroo
off (off the menu)	não há	naowng ah
off (switched)	desligado	dezleegahdoo
office	escritório, o	eshkreetoreeoo, o
OK	ok	oh keh
on	ligado	leegahdoo
once	uma vez	ooma vaysh
only	apenas	apehnash
open	aberto	abairtoo
to open	abrir	abreer
operator	operador, o	ohperadoor, o
opposite (place)	oposto	oposhtoo
optician's	oculista, o	okooleeshta, o
or	ou	oh
to order	encomendar	engkomengdar
other	outro/a	ooutroo/a
out of order	fora de serviço	fohra d serrveesoo
outdoor	exterior	ishtereeohr
outside	lá fora	lah fohra
overnight	pernoitar	pemoeetar
owner	dono/a, o/a	dohnoo/a, o/a
oxygen	oxigénio, o	oxeezheneeoo, o

P

painkiller	analgésico, o	analzhezeekoo, o
pair	par, o	parr, o
parents	pais, os	paeesh, osh
park	parque, o	parrk, o
to park	estacionar	ishtasseeonar
parking	estacionamento, o	ishtaseeonamengtoo, o

party	**festa, a**	*feshta, a*
passport	**passaporte, o**	*passaport, o*
to pay	**pagar**	*pagar*
people	**pessoas, as**	*peshoash, ash*
perhaps	**talvez**	*talvaysh*
person	**pessoa, a**	*peshoa, a*
phone	**telefone, o**	*telefon, o*
to phone	**telefonar**	*telefonar*
photo	**fotografia, a**	*fotgrafeea, a*
phrase book	**guia de conversação, o**	*gheea d congversasaowng, o*
place	**local, o**	*lookal, o*
platform	**plataforma, a**	*plataforma, a*
police	**polícia, o**	*polleeseea, o*

---

port (drink)   **vinho do porto, o**   *veenyoo doo portoo, o*

Vintage port is wine from a single harvest, bottled after two or three years. The best varieties then mature for at least a decade.

---

port (sea)	**porto, o**	*portoo, o*
Portugal	**Portugal**	*poortoogal*
Portuguese	**Português**	*poortooghaysh*
possible	**possível**	*posseevel*
post	**correio, o**	*koorayoo, o*
post office	**estação de correios, a**	*ishtasaowng d koorayoosh, a*
to prefer	**preferir**	*prefereer*

---

prescription   **receita médica, a**   *resayeeta medeeka, a*

Pharmacies and health shops sell aspirin and other simple drugs without prescriptions.

---

pretty	**bonito/a**	*booneetoo/a*
price	**preço, o**	*pressoo, o*
private	**privado**	*preevahdoo*
probably	**provavelmente**	*proovavelmengt*
problem	**problema, o**	*prooblayma*
pub	**bar, o**	*barr, o*
public transport	**transporte público, o**	*transhport poobleekoo, o*
to put	**colocar**	*koolookar*

Q

quality	**qualidade**	*kwaleedahd*
quantity	**quantidade**	*kwanteedahd*
quarter	**quarto, um**	*kwartoo, oom*
query	**pergunta, a**	*pairgoongta, a*
question	**pergunta, a**	*pairgoongta, a*

---

queue   **fila, a**   *feela, a*

The Portuguese form organised queues. Numbered tickets (**senhas**) are supplied at post offices, pharmacies and many other places to avoid any confusion.

| quick | **rápido** | *rappeedoo* |

quickly	**rapidamente**	*rappeedamengt*
quiet	**silencioso**	*seelengseeohzoo*
quite	**bastante**	*bashtangt*
quiz	**concurso, o**	*kongkoorsoo, o*

R

radio	**rádio, o**	*rahdioo*
railway	**caminho de ferro, o**	*kameenyoo d ferroo, o*

rain	**chuva, a**	*shoova, a*

Most rain falls in January, February and March. The northern areas are the dampest.

rape	**violação, a**	*veeolasaowng, a*
razor blade	**lâmina de barbear, a**	*lameena d barbayar, a*
ready	**pronto**	*prongtoo*
real	**verdadeiro/a**	*verdadayeeroo/a*
receipt	**recibo, o**	*reseeboo, o*
to receive	**receber**	*resebayr*
reception	**recepção, a**	*resepsaowng*
receptionist	**recepcionista, o/a**	*resepsioneesta, o/a*
to recommend	**recomendar**	*rekomendar*
reduction	**desconto, o**	*deshkongtoo, o*
refund	**reembolso, o**	*reengbolsoo, o*
to refuse	**recusar**	*rekoosar*
to relax	**relaxar**	*relashar*
rent	**renda, a**	*rengda, a*
to rent	**alugar**	*aloogar*
to request	**requerir**	*rekereer*
reservation	**reserva, a**	*rezerrva, a*
to reserve	**reservar**	*rezerrvar*
retired	**reformado**	*rezformahdoo*
rich	**rico**	*reekoo*
to ride	**andar de**	*angdar d*
right	**direita**	*deerayta*
to be right	**estar certo/a**	*ishtar sairtoo/a*
to ring	**telefonar**	*telfoonar*
road	**estrada, a**	*ishtrahda, a*
to rob	**roubar**	*ro-oubar*
room	**quarto, o**	*kwartoo, o*
route	**rota, a**	*roota, a*
rude	**grosseiro**	*groossayeeroo*
ruins	**ruínas, as**	*rooeenash, ash*
to run	**correr**	*koorrayr*

S

sad	**triste**	*treesht*
safe	**seguro**	*segooro*
sailing boat	**barco à vela, o**	*barrkoo a vehla, o*
sanitary towel	**toalha, a**	*tooalya, a*
sauna	**sauna, a**	*saoona, a*
Scotland	**escócia**	*ishkosseea*
Scottish	**escocês/esa, o/a**	*ishkoosaysh, o/a*
sea	**mar, o**	*mar, o*
seat	**lugar, o**	*loogar, o*

seat belt	cinto de segurança, o	*seengtoo, d segoorangsa, o*
sedative	sedativo, o	*sedateevoo, o*
see you later	até logo	*ateh logoo*
self-service	self-service	*self-serrvees*
to sell	vender	*vengdayr*
to send	enviar	*engveear*
sensible	sensível	*sengseevel*
September	Setembro	*setengbroo*
to serve	servir	*serrveer*
service	serviço, o	*serrveesoo, o*
shaving cream	creme de barbear, o	*krem d barrbayar, o*
shop	loja, a	*lohzha, a*
shop assistant	lojista, o/a	*lozheesta, o/a*
shopping	ir às compras	*eer d kongprash*
shopping centre	centro-comercial, o	*sengtroo-coomehrseeal, o*
short	pequeno	*pekenyoo*
shortage	falta de	*falta d*
short cut	atalho, o	*atalyoo, o*
show	espectáculo, o	*ishpetakooloo, o*
to show	mostrar	*mooshtrar*
shower	chuveiro, o	*shoovayeeroo, o*
shut	fechado	*feshahdoo*
sign	sinal, o	*sinal, o*
to sign	assinar	*asseenar*
signature	assinatura, a	*asseenatoora, a*
since	desde	*dezhd*
sir	senhor	*senyoor*
sister	irmã, a	*eermang, a*
ski	ski, o	*skee, o*
to sleep	dormir	*dohrmeer*
sleeping pill	comprimido para dormir, o	*kongpreemeedoo para dohrmeer, o*
slow	devagar	*devagar*
small	pequeno	*pekenyoo*
to smoke	fumar	*foomar*
soft	macio	*mahseeoo*
some	algum	*algoong*
something	alguma coisa	*algoonga koyza*
son	filho, o	*feelyoo, o*
soon	brevemente	*brevmengt*
south	sul	*sool*
South Africa	África do sul	*afreeka doo sool*
South African	Sul africano/a,	*sool afreekanoo/a*

speed	**velocidade, a**	***velohseedahd*, a**

Many Portuguese drivers drive excessively fast. Speed limits are 120 kph on motorways, 60 in built-up areas and 90 elsewhere.

to spell	soletrar	*sooletrar*
sport	desporto, o	*deshpohrtoo, o*
stadium	estádio, o	*ishtahdioo, o*
staff	pessoal, o	*pessooal, o*

stain	nódoa, a	nohdooa, o
stairs	escadas, as	ishkahdash, ash
stamp	selo, o	sehloo, o
to start	começar	coomesar
to start (car)	ligar	leegar
station	estação, a	ishtasaowng, a
stationer's	papelaria, a	papleareea, a
sterling pound	libra, a	leebra, a
to stop	parar	parrar
straight	direito	deerayeetoo
street	rua, a	rooa, a
stress	stress, o	shtress, o
suddenly	de repente	d repengt
suitcase	mala, a	mala, a
sun	sol, o	sol, o
sunglasses	óculos escuros, os	ohkooloos ishkoorosh, osh
surname	apelido, o	apeleedoo, o
swimming pool	piscina, a	pishceena, a
symptom	sintoma, o	seengtoma, o

T

table	mesa, a	mayza, a
to take	tomar/levar	toomar/lehvar
tall	alto/a	altoo/a
tampons	tampões, os	tangpongsh, osh
tax	imposto, o	imposhtoo, o
tax free	sem taxas	seng taksash
taxi	táxi, o	taksee, o
taxi rank	paragem de táxis, a	parazheng d takseesh, a
telephone	telefone, o	telefon, o
telephone box	cabine telefónica, a	kabeen telefonika, a
television	televisão, a	televeezaowng, a
tennis	ténis, o	tennees, o
terrace	terraço, o	terrassoo, o
to text	enviar uma mensagem escritar	engveear ooma mengsahzheng ishkreetar
that	aquilo	akeeloo
theft	roubo, o	roouboo, o
then	então	engtaowng
there	aí	ayee
thing	coisa, a	koeezha, a
to think	pensar	pengsar
thirsty	(tenho) sede	tenyoo sed
this	isto	ishtoo
through	através	atravesh
ticket (bus)	bilhete de autocarro, o	beelyayt d aootokarroo, o
ticket (cinema)	bilhete de cinema, o	beelyayt d seenayma, o
ticket (parking)	multa de estacionamento, a	moolta dishtaseenamengtoo, a
ticket (shopping)	recibo, o	resseeboo, o
ticket office	bilheteira, a	beelyaytayeera, a

time	tempo, o	tengpoo, o
time (clock)	horas, as	ohrash, osh
timetable	horário, o	ohrahreeo, o
tip (money)	gorgeta, a	gorzheta, a
tired	cansado/a	kansahdoo/a
to	para	para

| tobacco | tabaco, o | tabakoo, o |

Smoking is more acceptable here than in the UK, particularly in restaurants.

tobacconist's	tabaqueira, a	tabakayeera, a
today	hoje	ohzh
toilet	lavabos	lavahboosh
toiletries	artigos de banho, os	arteegoosh d banyoo, osh
toll	portagem, a	portahzheng, a
tomorrow	amanhã	amanyang
tonight	hoje à noite	ohzh ah noyt
too	também	tangbeng
tourist office	posto de turismo, o	poshtoo d tooreezmoo, o
town	vila, a	veela, a
town hall	câmara municipal, a	kahmara mooneeseepal, a
train	comboio, o	kongboyoo, o
tram	eléctrico, o	elektreekoo, o
to translate	traduzir	tradoozeer
travel	viajar	veeazhar
travel agency	agência de viagens, a	azhengseea d veeazhengs, a
true	verdadeiro	verrdahdayeeroo
typical	típico	teepeekoo

U

| ugly | feio | fayoo |
| ulcer | úlcera, a | oolsayra, a |

| umbrella | chapéu de chuva, o | shapayoo d shoova, o |

The Portuguese term for "umbrella" translates literally as "rain hat"!

uncomfortable	desconfortável	deshkongtahvel
unconcious	inconsciente	inkongshiengt
under	debaixo	debyzhoo
underground (tube)	Metropolitano (Metro), o	metroopoleetahnoo (metroo), o
to understand	perceber	perrsebayr
underwear	roupa interior, a	rooupa eentereeoor, a
unemployed	desempregado/a	dezengpreegahdoo/a
unpleasant	desagradável	dezagredahvel
up	para cima	para seema
upstairs	lá em cima	lah eng seema
urgent	urgente	oorzhengt
to use	usar	oozar

| useful | útil | ooteel |
| usually | normalmente | normalmengt |

V

vacant	vago	vahgoo
vacation	férias, as	faireeash, ash
vaccination	vacina, a	vaseena, a
valid	válido	valleedo
valuables	bens valiosos	bengsh valeeohzoosh
value	valor, o	valohr, o
VAT	IVA	eeva

| **vegetarian** | **vegetariano** | *vezhetareeahnoo* |

Big cities boast good vegetarian restaurants, and ordinary restaurants are serving more meat-free dishes.

vehicle	veículo, o	vayeekooloo, o
very	muito	mweetoo
visa	visa, a	veeza, a
visit	visita, a	veezeeta, a
to visit	visitar	veezeetar
vitamin	vitamina, a	veetameena, a
to vomit	vomitar	vomeetar

W

waiter/waitress	empregado/a, o/a	engpredooroo/a, o/a
waiting room	sala de espera, a	sahla d ishpaira, a
Wales	País de Gâles	paeess d gallesh
to walk	andar	angdar
wallet	carteira, a	kartayeera,a
to want	querer	kerrayr
to wash	lavar	laavar
watch	relógio, o	relozhoo, o
to watch	ver	vayr
water	água, a	ahgua, a
water sports	desportos aquáticos, os	deshportoosh akwateekosh, os
way (manner)	modo, o	mohdoo, o
way (route)	caminho, o	kameenyoo, o
way in	entrada, a	engtrahda, a
way out	saída, a	sayeeda, a
weather	tempo, o	tengpoo, o
web	web	web
website	website	webseet
week	semana, a	semahna, a
weekday	dia da semana, o	deea d semahna, o
weekend	fim de semana, o	fing d semahna, o
welcome	bem-vindo/a	bengveengdoo/a
well	bem	beng
well done	muito bem	mweetoo beng
Welsh	Galês/esa	galesh/eza
west	oeste, o	ooesht, o
what?	o quê?	o keh?
wheelchair	cadeira de rodas, a	kadayeera de rohdash, a

when?	**quando?**	*kwangdoo?*
where?	**onde?**	*ongd?*
which?	**qual?**	*kwal?*
while	**enquanto**	*engkwangtoo*
who?	**quem?**	*keng?*
why?	**porquê?**	*poorkeh?*

| wife | **esposa, a** | *ishpohza, a* |

Esposa is the formal term for wife. But in everyday speech, people use **mulher** (woman), as in "**minha mulher**" (my wife).

to win	**ganhar**	*ganyar*
with	**com**	*kong*
without	**sem**	*seng*
woman	**mulher, a**	*moolyair*
wonderful	**maravilhoso**	*maraveelyoosoo*
word	**palavra, a**	*palavra, a*
work	**trabalho, o**	*trabalyoo, o*
to work	**trabalhar**	*trabalyar*
world	**mundo, o**	*moongdo*
worried	**preocupado/a**	*preokoopahdoo/a*
worse	**pior**	*peyor*
to write	**escrever**	*ishkrever*
wrong (mistaken)	**enganado/a**	*enganahdoo/a*

X

xenophobe	**xenófobo/a, o/a**	*shenohfobo/a, o/a*
xenophobia	**xenofobia**	*shenofobeea*
x-ray	**radiografia, a**	*radeeografeea, a*
to x-ray	**tirar uma radiografia**	*teerar ooma radeeografeea*

Y

yacht	**iate, o**	*yatte, o*
year	**ano, o**	*ahnoo, o*
yearly	**anualmente**	*anooalmengt*
yellow pages	**páginas amarelas, as**	*pazheenash amarehlash, ash*
yes	**sim**	*seeng*
yesterday	**ontem**	*ongteng*
yet	**ainda**	*aeengda*
you (formal)	**você**	*vossay*
you (informal)	**tu**	*too*
young	**jovem**	*zhoveng*
your (formal)	**vosso**	*vossoo*
your (informal)	**teu**	*tayoo*
youth hostel	**pousada da juventude, a**	*po-oussahda da zhoovengtood, a*

Z

zebra crossing	**passagem de peões, a**	*passahzheng d peongsh, a*
zip	**fecho eclair, o**	*fayshoo eklair, o*
zone	**zona, a**	*zohna, a*
zoo	**jardim zoológico, o**	*zhardeem zoo-oolozheekoo, o*

Portuguese-English dictionary

A

abastecimento	*abasheseemengtoo*	filling (station)
aberto	*abairtoo*	open
Abril	*abreel*	April
abrir	*abreer*	to open
acabar	*akabar*	to finish
acidente, o	*aseedengt*	accident
advogado/a, o/a	*advoogahdoo/a, o/a*	lawyer
aeroporto, o	*aehrooportoo, o*	airport
África do sul	*afreeka doo sool*	South Africa
agência de câmbio, a	*azhengseea d kambeeoo, a*	bureau de change
agência de viagens, a	*azhengseea d veeahzhengs, a*	travel agency
agora	*agohra*	now
Agosto	*agoshtoo*	August

água, a	*ahgua, a*	water

Portuguese tap water is safe to drink, but not always palatable.

aí	*ayee*	there
ainda	*aeengda*	yet
ajudar	*azhoodar*	to help
alarme, o	*alahrrm, o*	alarm
alarme de incêndios, o	*alarrm d eensengdeeoosh, o*	fire alarm
alergia, a	*alairzheea, a*	allergy
alfândega, a	*alfangdega, a*	customs

alforeca, a	*alforehka, a*	jellyfish

Portuguese men-of-war are actually not jellyfish, but rather a colony of polyps.

algum	*algoong*	some
alguma coisa	*algoonga koyza*	something
alojamento, o	*aloozhamentoo*	accommodation
alto/a	*altoo/a*	high, tall
alugar	*aloogar*	to hire, rent
amanhã	*amanyang*	tomorrow
ambulância, a	*angboolangshia, a*	ambulance
América	*ameyreeka*	America
Americano/a	*ameyreekahnoo/a*	American
amigo/a, o/a	*ameegoo/a, o/a*	friend
analgésico, o	*analzhezeekoo, o*	painkiller
andar	*angdar*	to walk
andar de	*angdar d*	to ride
aniversário, o	*aneeversahreeoo, o*	anniversary
ano, o	*ahnoo, o*	year
antes	*antesh*	before
anualmente	*anooalmengt*	yearly
ao lado de	*aow lahdoo d*	by (beside)

apartamento, o	apartamengtoo	apartment
apelido, o	apeleedoo, o	surname
apenas	apehnash	only
aqui	akee	here
aquilo	akeeloo	that
área, a	ahreea, a	area
arranjar	arrangzhar	to get
arte	arrt	art
artigos de banho, os	arteegoosh d banyoo, osh	toiletries
aspirina, a	aspeereena, a	aspirin
assinar	asseenar	to sign
assinatura, a	asseenatoora, a	signature
atalho, o	atalyoo, o	short cut
até logo	ateh logoo	see you later
atenção	atensaowng	attention
atrasado/a	atrassahdoo/a	late (delayed)
atrás de	atrash d	behind
atraso	atrassoo	delay
através	atravesh	through
Austrália	aooshtrahleea	Australia
Australiano/a	aooshtrahleeahnoo/a	Australian
autocarro, o	aowtookarro, o	bus
avião, o	aveeaowng, o	aeroplane

B

bagagem, a	bahgahzheng, a	baggage, luggage
banheira, a	banyayeera, a	bath
bar, o	bahr, o	bar (pub)
barato	barahtoo	cheap
barco à vela, o	barrkoo a vehla, o	sailing boat
bastante	bashtangt	quite
bater	batayr	to knock
bebé, o	behbeh, o	baby
beijar	bayeezhar	to kiss
beijo, o	bayeezhoo, o	kiss
bem	beng	well
bem-vindo/a	bengveengdoo/a	welcome
bens valiosos	bengsh valeeohzoosh	valuables
berço, o	bairsoo, o	cot
biblioteca, a	beebliooteka, a	library
bicicleta, a	beeseekleta, a	bicycle
bilhete de autocarro, o	beelyayt d aootokarroo, o	ticket (bus)
bilhete de cinema, o	beelyayt d seenayma, o	ticket (cinema)
bilhete de identidade, o	beelyet d eedengtidahd, o	identity card
bilheteira, a	beelyetayeera, a	box/ticket office
bocado, um	bookahdoo, oong	bit (a)
bom/boa	bong/boa	good, nice
bonito/a	booneetoo/a	pretty
brevemente	brevmengt	soon

cabeleireiro, o	*kabellayrayeeroo, o*	hairdresser's
cabelo, o	*kabelloo, o*	hair
cabine telefónica, a	*kabeen telefonika, a*	telephone box
cabrito, o	*kabreetoo, o*	kid (meat)
cadeira de rodas, a	*kadayeera de rohdash, a*	wheelchair
café, o	*kaffeh, o*	café
caixa de Multibanco, a	*kysha d mooltee-bangkoo, a*	cash point
calor, o	*kalohr, o*	heat
câmara municipal, a	*kahmara mooneeseepal, a*	town hall
caminho, o	*kameenyoo, o*	way (route)
caminho de ferro, o	*kameenyoo d ferroo, o*	railway
campo, o	*kampoo, o*	countryside
cancelar	*kanselar*	to cancel
cansado/a	*kansahdoo/a*	tired
carro, o	*karroo, o*	car
carta, a	*karrta, a*	letter
cartão de crédito, o	*kartaowng de kredeet, o*	credit card
cartão de embarque, o	*kartaowng d embarrke, o*	boarding card
carteira, a	*kartayeera,a*	wallet
casado/a	*cazahdoo/a*	married
CD, o	*se de, o*	cd
cedo	*saydoo*	early
centro, o	*sentroo, o*	centre
centro-comercial, o	*sengtroo-koomehrseeal, o*	shopping centre
chamar	*shamar*	to call
chapéu de chuva, o	*shapayoo d shoova, o*	umbrella
charuto, o	*sharootoo, o*	cigar
chave, a	*shav, a*	key
chegada	*shegahda*	arrival
cheque, o	*sheke, o*	cheque
chuva, a	*shoova, a*	rain
chuveiro, o	*shoovayeeroo, o*	shower

cidade, a	***seedahd, a***	**city**

Lisbon has been the country's capital since 1255.

cigarro, o	*seegarroo, o*	cigarette
cinema, o	*seenayma, o*	cinema
cinto de segurança, o	*seengtoo, d segoorangsa, o*	seat belt
clube, o	*kloob,o*	club
cobrar	*koobrar*	to charge
coisa, a	*koeezha, a*	thing
colete de salvação, o	*kolette d salvasaowng, o*	life jacket
colocar	*koolookar*	to put
com	*kong*	with
combinar	*kongbeenar*	to arrange
comboio, o	*kongboyoo, o*	train

começar	*coomesar*	to start

comer	*comayr*	**to eat**

Don't go home without trying a custard tart sprinkled
with cinnamon – delicious.

como?	*koomoo?*	how?
comprar	*koomprar*	to buy
comprimido para dormir, o	*kongpreemeedoo para dohrmeer, o*	sleeping pill
concurso, o	*kongkoorsoo, o*	quiz
conduzir	*kongdoozeer*	to drive
confirmação, a	*kongfeermasaowng*	confirmation
confirmar	*kongfeermar*	to confirm
conhecer	*koonyesayr*	to know (person)
consulado, o	*konsoolahdoo, o*	consulate
conta, a	*kongta, a*	bill
contactar	*kontaktar*	to contact
contagioso	*kongtazheeozoo*	contagious
cor, a	*kohr, a*	colour
correio, o	*koorayoo, o*	mail, post
correr	*koorrayr*	to run
cortar	*korrtar*	to cut
corte, o	*korrt, o*	cut
costa, a	*koshta, a*	coast
creme de barbear, o	*krem d barrbayar, o*	shaving cream
criança, a	*kreeangsa, a*	child
crime, o	*kreem, o*	crime
custar	*kooshtar*	to cost
custo	*kooshtoo*	charge
custo, o	*kooshtoo, o*	cost

D

danos	*danoosh*	damage
dar	*dahr*	to give
data, a	*dahta, a*	date (calendar)
de	*d*	by (via), from
de (de avião, carro, etc)	*d (d aveeaowng, carroo, etc.)*	by (by air, car, etc)
de casal	*d kazal*	double (room, bed)
de que tamanho?	*d k tamanyoo*	how big?
de repente	*d repengt*	suddenly
debaixo	*debyzhoo*	under
deficiente	*defeeseeyengt*	disabled
dentro	*dengtroo*	inside
depois	*depoysh*	after
depressa!	*depressa!*	hurry up!
desagradável	*dezagredahvel*	unpleasant
desaparecido/a	*dezapareseedoo/a*	missing
desconfortável	*deshkongtahvel*	uncomfortable

desconto, o	*deshkongtoo, o*	**discount**

The Lisboa card offers free entry to 25 museums and
monuments, as well as unlimited public transport.

desde	*dezhd*	since
desempregado/a	*dezengpreegahdoo/a*	unemployed
desidratar	*dezeedratar*	to dehydrate
desinfectante, o	*dezeenfektangt, o*	disinfectant
desligado	*dezleegahdoo*	off (switched)
desporto, o	*deshpohrtoo, o*	sport
desportos aquáticos, os	*deshportoosh akwateekosh, os*	water sports
devagar	*devagar*	slow
deve	*dehv*	must
Dezembro	*dezhengbroo*	December
dia da semana, o	*deea d semahna, o*	weekday
dia, o	*deea, o*	day
difícil	*deefeesseel*	difficult
dinheiro, o	*deenyayeeroo, o*	money
direcções	*deereksongsh*	directions
direita	*deerayta*	right
direito	*deerayeetoo*	straight
discoteca, a	*deeskotehka, a*	disco, nightclub
disfrutar	*deeshfrootar*	to enjoy
disponível	*deeshpooneevel*	available
doente	*dooengt*	ill
doer	*dooayr*	to hurt
dono/a, o/a	*dohnoo/a, o/a*	owner
dormir	*dohrmeer*	to sleep
droga, a	*drohga, a*	drug
durante	*doorant*	during
durante quanto tempo?	*doorangt kwangtoo tengpoo?*	how long?

E

e	*e*	and
é muito longe?	*eh mweetoo longzhe?*	how far?
eléctrico, o	*elektreekoo, o*	tram
em	*eng*	in, at
em casa	*eng kahza*	at home
em dinheiro	*eng deenyayeeroo*	cash
em lado nenhum	*eng lahdoo nenyoong*	nowhere
e-mail, o	*emmayl, o*	e-mail
embaixada, a	*engbaeeshahda, a*	embassy
emergência, a	*emerrzhengseea, a*	emergency
empregado/a, o/a	*engpredooroo/a, o/a*	waiter/waitress
encomendar	*engkomengdar*	to order
enganado/a	*enganahdoo/a*	wrong (mistaken)
enquanto	*engkwangtoo*	while
então	*engtaowng*	then
entrada, a	*engtrahda, a*	way in
entre	*entr*	between
entroncamento, o	*engtronkamengtoo, o*	junction
enviar	*engveear*	to send
enviar um fax	*engveear oom fax*	to fax
enviar uma mensagem escritar	*engveear ooma mengsahzheng ishkreetar*	to text
erro, o	*erroo, o*	error

escadas, as	*ishkahdash, ash*	stairs
escocês/esa, o/a	*ishkoosaysh, o/a*	Scottish
escócia	*ishkosseea*	Scotland
escrever	*ishkrever*	to write
escritório, o	*eshkreetoreeoo, o*	office
escutar	*eshkootar*	to listen to
espectáculo, o	*ishpetakooloo, o*	show
esposa, a	*ishpohza, a*	wife
esquerdo/a	*eshkehrdoo/a*	left
estação, a	*ishtasaowng, a*	station
estação de correios, a	*ishtasaowng d koorayoosh, a*	post office
estacionamento, o	*ishtaseeonamengtoo, o*	parking
estacionar	*ishtasseeonar*	to park
estádio, o	*ishtahdioo, o*	stadium
estar certo/a	*ishtar sairtoo/a*	to be right
estrada, a	*ishtrahda, a*	road
exportar	*ishpoortar*	to export
exposição, a	*ishpoozeesaowng, a*	exhibition
expresso	*ishpressoo*	express (delivery)
expresso, o	*ishpressoo, o*	express (train)
exterior	*ishtereeohr*	outdoor

F

falta de	*falta d*	shortage
fazer	*fazhayr*	to make
fazer o checkin	*fazayr o shekin*	to check in
fechado/a	*feshadoo/a*	closed
fechar	*feshar*	to close
fecho eclair, o	*fayshoo eklair, o*	zip
feio	*fayoo*	ugly
feriado, o	*ferreeahdoo, o*	holiday (bank holiday)
férias, as	*faireeash, ash*	holidays
festa, a	*feshta, a*	party
Fevereiro	*feverayeeroo*	February
fila, a	*feela, a*	queue
filha, a	*feelya, a*	daughter
filho, o	*feelyoo, o*	son
filme, o	*feelm, o*	film (cinema)
fim de semana, o	*fing d semahna, o*	weekend
finalmente	*feenalmengt*	at last
fogo, o	*foogoo, o*	fire
fora	*fohra*	away
fora de serviço	*fohra d serrveesoo*	out of order
formulário, o	*formoolahreeoo, o*	form (document)
fotografia, a	*fotografeea, a*	photo
fresco	*frayshkoo*	cool
frio	*freeoo*	cold
fumar	*foomar*	to smoke
futebol, o	*footebol, o*	football

G

galeria, a	*galereea, a*	gallery
Galês/esa	*galesh/eza*	Welsh
ganhar	*ganyar*	to win

garagem, a	_garahzheng, a_	garage
garantia, a	_garangteea, a_	guarantee
gás, o	_gass, o_	gas
gerente, o	_zherengt, o_	manager

golfe, o	_golfe, o_	golf

The Algarve has some of Europe's best courses, including the exclusive San Lorenzo and Quinta do Lago.

gorgeta, a	_gorzheta, a_	tip (money)
gostar	_gooshtar_	to like
grande	_grangd_	big
grátis	_grahtees_	free (money)
gripe, a	_greep, a_	flu
grosseiro	_groossayeeroo_	rude
grupo, o	_groopoo, o_	group
guardar	_gwarrdar_	to keep
guia, o	_gheea, a_	guide
guia de conversação, o	_gheea d congversasaowng, o_	phrase book

H

há	_ah_	ago
hoje	_ohzh_	today
hoje à noite	_ohzh ah noyt_	tonight
homem, o	_ohmeng, o_	man
homens	_ohmengs_	gents
homosexual, o	_omoseksooal, o_	homosexual
horário, o	_ohrahreeo, o_	timetable
horas, as	_ohrash, osh_	time (clock)
hospital, o	_ospeetal, o_	hospital

I

| iate, o | _yatte, o_ | yacht |
| igreja, a | _eegrayzha, a_ | church |

ilha, a	_eelya, a_	island

The Azores islands, in the middle of the Atlantic Ocean, have a great history and natural beauty.

imediatamente	_eemaydeeatamengt_	at once
importante	_eemportangt_	important
importar	_eemportar_	to import
imposto, o	_imposhtoo, o_	tax
inconsciente	_inkongshiengt_	unconscious
indicativo	_eengdeekateevoo_	area code
informação, a	_eenformasaowng, a_	information
Inglaterra	_eenglaterra_	England
Inglês/esa	_eenglesh/ingleza_	English
instalações, as	_eengshtalasoesh, ash_	facilities
interessante	_interressangt_	interesting
internacional	_interrnaseeonal_	international
intoxicação alimentar, a	_eengtoxikasaowng aleemengtar, a_	food poisoning

ir	*eer*	to go
ir às compras	*eer d kongprash*	shopping
Irlanda	*eerlangda*	Ireland
Irlandês/esa	*eerlangdaysh/dayza*	Irish
irmã, a	*eermang, a*	sister
irmão, o	*eermaowng, o*	brother
isto	*ishtoo*	this
itinerário, o	*eeteenerahreeoo, o*	itinerary
IVA	*eeva*	VAT

J

já	*zha*	immediately
Janeiro	*zhanayeeroo*	January
jardim zoológico, o	*zhardeem zoo-oolozheekoo, o*	zoo
jet-ski, o	*zhet-skee, o*	jet ski
jornal, o	*zhornal, o*	newspaper
jovem	*zhoveng*	young
Julho	*zhoolyoo*	July

| **Junho** | ***zhoonyoo*** | **June** |

Portugal's countrywide June celebrations have pagan roots but have since been dedicated to three popular saints: Anthony, John and Peter.

L

lá em cima	*lah eng seema*	upstairs
lá fora	*lah fohra*	outside
lâmina de barbear, a	*lameena d barbayar, a*	razor blade
lavabos	*lavahboosh*	toilet
lavandaria, a	*lavandareea, a*	launderette, dry-cleaner's
lavar	*laavar*	to wash
levantar	*levantar*	lift
libra, a	*leebra, a*	sterling pound
ligado	*leegahdoo*	on
ligar	*leegar*	to start (car)
língua, a	*leengwa, a*	language
livre	*leevr*	free (vacant)
local	*lookal*	local

| **livro, o** | ***leevroo, o*** | **book** |

Lisbon's Praça do Comério is turned into an open-air book fair in May–June.

local, o	*lookal, o*	place
loja, a	*lohzha, a*	shop
lojista, o/a	*lozheesta, o/a*	shop assistant
longe	*longzh*	far
lugar, o	*loogar, o*	seat

M

| macio | *mahseeoo* | soft |

mãe, a	_myng, a_	mother
Maio	_mahyoo_	May
maioria, a	_mayooreea, a_	most
mais	_mash_	more
mala, a	_mala, a_	suitcase
mapa da cidade, o	_mapa da seedahd, o_	map (city)
mapa das estradas, o	_mapa dash eshtrahdash_	map (road)
máquina fotográfica, a	_makeena fotografeeka, a_	camera

mar, o	**_mar, o_**	**sea**

Lisbon's spectacular steel-and-glass Oceanário is Europe's biggest.

maravilhoso	_maraveelyoosoo_	wonderful
marcação, a	_markasaowng, a_	appointment
marcar	_marrkar_	to dial
Março	_marrsoo_	March
marido, o	_mareedoo, o_	husband
mas	_mash_	but
matar	_mattar_	to kill
mecânico, o	_mekaneekoo, o_	mechanic
médico, o	_mehdeekoo, o_	doctor
meio/a	_meeyoo/a_	half
meia-noite	_meeya-noyt_	midnight
meio-dia	_meeyoo-deea_	midday
melhor, o/a	_melyor, o/a_	best
melhor que	_melyor k_	better
menos	_menoosh_	less
mensagem, a	_mengsahzheng, a_	message

mercado, o	**_maircahdoo, o_**	**market**

Portimão is home to one of Portugal's best fish markets, and is a great place to buy souvenirs.

mesa, a	_mayza, a_	table
Metropolitano (Metro), o	_metroopoleetahnoo (metroo), o_	underground (tube)
meu/minha	_mayoo/meenya_	my
minha senhora	_meenya senyoora_	madam
mínimo, o	_meeneenoo, o_	minimum
minuto, o	_meenootoo, o_	minute
modo, o	_mohdoo, o_	way (manner)
moeda, a	_mooehda, a_	currency
momento, o	_moomentoo, o_	moment
mosquito, o	_mooshkeetoo, o_	mosquito
mostrar	_mooshtrar_	to show
motorista, o	_motoreesta, o_	driver
mudar	_moodar_	to change
muito	_mweetoo_	much, very
muito bem	_mweetoo beng_	well done
muitos	_mweetoosh_	many
mulher, a	_moolyair, a_	woman

| multa de estacionamento, a | *moolta dishtaseena-mengtoo, a* | ticket (parking) |
| mundo, o | *moongdo* | world |

| **museu, o** | ***moozayoo, o*** | **museum** |

Queen Leonor Museum in Beja is home to valuable archaeological finds.

N

nacionalidade, a	*nasseeonaleedahd, a*	nationality
nada	*nahda*	nothing
não há	*naowng ah*	off (off the menu)
natas, as	*nahtash, ash*	cream
necessário	*nessesahrioo*	necessary
negócios	*negoseeosh*	business
nódoa, a	*nohdooa, o*	stain
noite, a	*noyt, a*	night
nome, o	*nohm, o*	name
normalmente	*normalmengt*	usually
norte, o	*nort, o*	north
nota, a	*nota, a*	note (money)
notícias, as	*nooteesheeash, ash*	news
Novembro	*noovembroo*	November
novo	*noovoo*	new
número, o	*noomehroo, o*	number
nunca	*noongka*	never

O

o quê?	*o keh?*	what?
objecto, o	*obzhetoo, o*	object
objectos perdidos, os	*obzhetoosh perdee-doosh*	lost property
oculista, o	*okooleeshta, o*	optician's
óculos, os	*okkoolosh, osh*	glasses
óculos escuros, os	*ohkooloos ishkoorosh, osh*	sunglasses

| **oeste, o** | ***ooesht, o*** | **west** |

The cliffs of Parque Natural de Sintra-Cascais are mainland Europe's westernmost point.

ok	*oh keh*	OK
olhar	*ohlyar*	to look
onde?	*ongd?*	where?
ontem	*ongteng*	yesterday
operador, o	*ohperadoor, o*	operator
oposto	*oposhtoo*	opposite (place)
ou	*oh*	or
outro/a	*ooutroo/a*	other, another
outra vez	*ooutra vaysh*	again
Outubro	*oooutoobroo*	October
oxigénio, o	*oxeezheneeoo, o*	oxygen

pagar	*pagar*	to pay
páginas amarelas, as	*pazheenash amarehlash, ash*	yellow pages
pai, o	*py, o*	father
país, o	*paeesh, o*	country
País de Gâles	*paeess d gallesh*	Wales
pais, os	*paeesh, osh*	parents
palavra, a	*palavra, a*	word
papelaria, a	*papleareea, a*	stationer's
par, o	*parr, o*	pair
para	*para*	to, for
para cima	*para seema*	up
parabéns!	*parabens*	congratulations!
paragem de autocarro, a	*parahgeng d aowtookarroo, a*	bus stop
paragem de táxis, a	*parazheng d takseesh, a*	taxi rank
parar	*parrar*	to stop

parque, o	*parrk, o*	park

Peneda Geres, the country's only national park, is one of the last refuges for wolves and royal eagles.

partir	*parteer*	to leave
passagem de peões, a	*passahzheng d peongsh, a*	zebra crossing
passaporte, o	*passaport, o*	passport
pelo menos	*payloo maynoosz*	at least
pensar	*pengsar*	to think
pequeno	*pekenyoo*	small, short
perceber	*perrsebayr*	to understand
perder	*pairdayr*	to miss, lose
pergunta, a	*pairgoongta, a*	question, query
perguntar	*pairgoongtar*	to ask
perigo, o	*pereegoo, o*	danger
pernoitar	*pemoeetar*	overnight
perto	*pairtoo*	near
perto de	*pairtoo d*	close by, next to
perturbar	*perrtoorbar*	to disturb
pessoa, a	*peshoa, a*	person
pessoal, o	*pessooal, o*	staff
pessoas, as	*peshoash, ash*	people
picada de mosquito, a	*peekahda d mooshkeetoo, a*	mosquito bite
pior	*peyor*	worse
piscina, a	*pishceena, a*	swimming pool
plataforma, a	*plataforma, a*	platform
poder	*poodayr*	can (to be able)
polícia, o	*polleeseea, o*	police
por avião	*pour aviaowng*	airmail
por baixo	*poor byshoo*	down
porque	*porrke*	because
porquê?	*poorkeh?*	why?
portagem, a	*portahzheng, a*	toll

| porto, o | *portoo, o* | port (sea) |
| Portugal | *poortoogal* | Portugal |

Português   *poortooghaysh*   **Portuguese**
During the 15th century, Portuguese was the most widely spoken language in the world.

possível	*posseevel*	possible
posto de turismo, o	*poshtoo d tooreezmoo, o*	tourist office
pouco/a	*pohkoo/a*	little (a little)
pousada da juventude, a	*po-oussahda da zhoovengtood, a*	youth hostel
praia, a	*prahyeea, a*	beach
praia de nudistas, a	*prya d noodeeshtash*	nudist beach
precisamente	*preseezamengt*	exactly
precisar	*presseezar*	to need
preço, o	*pressoo, o*	price
preferido/a	*prefereedoo/a*	favourite
preferir	*prefereer*	to prefer
preocupado/a	*preokoopahdoo/a*	worried
primeira classe	*preemayra klass*	business class
primeiros socorros	*preemayeeroosh sookoorroosh*	first aid
principal	*preenseepal*	main
privado	*preevahdoo*	private
problema, o	*prooblayma*	problem
pronto	*prongtoo*	ready
provadores	*proovadorrsh*	fitting room
provavelmente	*proovavelmengt*	probably

Q
qual?	*kwal?*	which?
qualidade	*kwaleedahd*	quality
qualquer	*kwalkair*	any
quando?	*kwangdoo?*	when?
quantidade	*kwanteedahd*	quantity
quanto?	*kwangtoo?*	how much?
quarto, o	*kwartoo, o*	room
quarto, um	*kwartoo, oom*	quarter

queimar   *kayeemar*   **to burn**
Forest fires in 2005 were the worst in living memory, affecting two-thirds of the country.

queixa, a	*kaysha, a*	complaint
queixar-se	*kayshar-se*	to complain
quem?	*keng?*	who?
quente	*kennt*	hot
querer	*kerrayr*	to want
quiosque, o	*keeoshk, o*	kiosk

R
| rádio, o | *rahdioo* | radio |
| radiografia, a | *radeeografeea, a* | x-ray |

rapariga, a	*rapareega, a*	girl
rapaz, o	*rapash, o*	boy
rapidamente	*rappeedamengt*	quickly
rápido	*rapeedoo*	quick, fast
receber	*resebayr*	to receive
receita médica, a	*resayeeta medeeka, a*	prescription
recepção, a	*resepsaowng*	reception
recepcionista, o/a	*resepsioneesta, o/a*	receptionist
recibo, o	*reseeboo, o*	receipt
recomendar	*rekomendar*	to recommend
recusar	*rekoosar*	to refuse
reembolso, o	*reengbolsoo, o*	refund
reformado	*rezformahdoo*	retired
relaxar	*relashar*	to relax
relógio, o	*relozhoo, o*	watch
renda, a	*rengda, a*	rent
requerir	*rekereer*	to request
reserva, a	*rezerrva, a*	booking, reservation
reservar	*rezerrvar*	to book, reserve
responder	*reshpondair*	to answer
reunião, a	*rayooniaowng, a*	meeting
rico	*reekoo*	rich
rolo fotográfico, o	*rooloo fotografeekoo, o*	film (camera)

| **rota, a** | **_roota, a_** | **route** |
| In northeast Alentejo, the Rota dos Castelos, or Castle Route, takes in a series of beautiful towns and villages. | | |

roubar	*ro-oubar*	to rob
roubo, o	*roouboo, o*	theft
roupa, a	*rooupa, a*	clothes
roupa interior, a	*rooupa eengtereeoor, a*	underwear
rua, a	*rooa, a*	street

| **ruínas, as** | **_rooeenash, ash_** | **ruins** |
| Conimbriga, 15km southwest of Coimbra, is home to the best-preserved Roman ruins in Portugal. | | |

S

saber	*sabayr*	to know (knowledge)
saída, a	*sayeeda, a*	way out
saída de emergência, a	*sayeeda d emerzhengseeya*	fire exit
sala de espera, a	*sahla d ishpaira, a*	waiting room
salvavidas, o	*salvaveedash., o*	lifeguard
sauna, a	*saoona, a*	sauna
sedativo, o	*sedateevoo, o*	sedative
sede	*sed*	thirsty
seguinte	*segeengt*	next
seguro	*segooro*	safe
seguro, o	*segooroo, o*	insurance
self-service	*self-serrvees*	self-service
selo, o	*sehloo, o*	stamp

sem	seng	without
sem taxas	seng taksash	tax free
semana, a	semahna, a	week
senhor	senyoor	sir
senhora, a	senyoora, a	lady
senhoras	senyoorash	ladies (toilets)
sensível	sengseevel	sensible
ser/estar	sehr/ishtar	to be
serviço, o	serrveesoo, o	service
servir	serrveer	to serve
Setembro	setengbroo	September
SIDA, a	seeda, a	AIDS

| **ski, o** | **skee, o** | **ski** |

The Serra da Estrala, Central Portugal, is the country's highest plateau, with skiing from January-March. It's also home to the country's rare mountain lizard.

silencioso	seelengseeohzoo	quiet
sim	seeng	yes
simpático/a	seengpatteekoo/a	kind (nice)
sinal, o	sinal, o	sign
sintoma, o	seengtoma, o	symptom
só	soh	just (only)
sobre	sobr	about (concerning)
socorro!	sokorroo!	help!
soletrar	sooletrar	to spell
stress, o	shtress, o	stress
suficiente	soofeeseyengt	enough
sujo/a	soozhoo/a	dirty
sul	sool	south
Sul africano/a,	sool afreekanoo/a	South African

T

tabaco, o	tabakoo, o	tobacco
tabaqueira, a	tabakayeera, a	tobacconist's
talvez	talvesh	maybe
também	tangbeng	too
tampões, os	tangpongsh, osh	tampons
tarde	tarrd	late (time)
taxa, a	tasha, a	duty (tax)
taxa de câmbio, a	tasha d kambeeoo, a	exchange rate
táxi, o	taksee, o	taxi
tecido, o	tesseedoo, o	material (cloth)
telefonar	telefonar	to phone
telefone, o	telefon, o	telephone

| **telemóvel, o** | **telemohvel, o** | **mobile phone** |

To avoid expensive roaming charges when using your mobile phone in Portugal, buy a local pay-as-you-go SIM card: local and national calls are then cheap and you pay nothing on incoming calls.

televisão, a	*televee<u>zao</u>wng, a*	television
tempo, o	*teng<u>poo</u>, o*	time, weather
ténis, o	*ten<u>nees</u>, o*	tennis
ter	*tayr*	to have
ter fome	*tayr fom*	to be hungry
terraço, o	*terr<u>ass</u>oo, o*	terrace
teu	*tay<u>oo</u>*	your (informal)
típico	*tee<u>pee</u>koo*	typical
tipo, o	*tee<u>poo</u>, o*	kind (sort)
tirar uma radiografia	*teer<u>ar</u> <u>oo</u>ma radeeograf<u>ee</u>a*	to x-ray
toalha, a	*too<u>alya</u>, a*	sanitary towel
tomar/levar	*toom<u>ar</u>/leh<u>var</u>*	to take

touca de banho, a	*<u>too</u>uka d <u>ban</u>yoo, a*	bathing cap

Bathing caps tend to be obligatory at Portugal's indoor swimming pools, as are flip flops. Come prepared!

trabalhar	*tra<u>bal</u>yar*	to work
trabalho, o	*tra<u>bal</u>yoo, o*	work
traduzir	*tradoo<u>zeer</u>*	to translate
transporte público, o	*transh<u>port</u> <u>poob</u>leekoo, o*	public transport
traseiras	*tra<u>zay</u>eerash*	back (place)
triste	*treesht*	sad
tu	*too*	you (informal)
tudo	*<u>too</u>doo*	all
tudo bem	*<u>too</u>doo beng*	all right

U

úlcera, a	*<u>ool</u>sayra, a*	ulcer
último/a	*<u>ool</u>teemoo/a*	last
um/uma	*oong/<u>oong</u>a*	a(n)
uma vez	*<u>oo</u>ma vaysh*	once
Urgências	*oor<u>zheng</u>seeyash*	A&E
urgente	*oor<u>zheng</u>t*	urgent
usar	*ooz<u>ar</u>*	to use
útil	*<u>oo</u>teel*	useful

V

vacina, a	*va<u>see</u>na, a*	vaccination
vago	*<u>vah</u>goo*	vacant
válido	*<u>val</u>leedo*	valid
valor, o	*val<u>ohr</u>, o*	value
vegetariano	*vezhetaree<u>ah</u>noo*	vegetarian
veículo, o	*va<u>yee</u>kooloo, o*	vehicle
velocidade, a	*velohsee<u>dah</u>d*	speed
vender	*veng<u>dayr</u>*	to sell
ver	*vayr*	to watch
verdadeiro/a	*verda<u>day</u>eeroo/a*	real, true
viagem, a	*vee<u>ahz</u>heng, a*	journey
viajar	*veeazh<u>ar</u>*	travel
vila, a	*<u>vee</u>la, a*	town

vinho do porto, o   _veen_yoo doo _por_too, o   port (drink)
Portuguese wines have been exported since Roman times.
Vinho Verde and fortified wines such as **Porto** and **Madeira**
are the best known. For something different, try the
renowned reds of the **Douro** or up-and-coming **Dâo**

violação, a	_veeolasaowng, a_	rape
vir	_veer_	to come
visa, a	_veeza, a_	visa
visita, a	_veezeeta, a_	visit
visitar	_veezeetar_	to visit
vitamina, a	_veetameena, a_	vitamin
você	_vossay_	you (formal)
vomitar	_vomeetar_	to vomit
voo, o	_vo_-oo, o	flight
vosso	_vossoo_	your (formal)

W
web	_web_	web

website   _web_seet   website
Check out www.visitportugal.com, the extensive website of
the Portuguese Tourist Institute.

X
xenófobo/a, o/a	_shenohfobo/a, o/a_	xenophobe
xenophobia	_shenofobeea_	xenophobia

Z
zero, o	_zairoo, o_	zero
zona, a	_zohna, a_	zone

Numbers

0	**zero**	_zairoo_
1	**um**	_oom_
2	**dois**	_doheesh_
3	**três**	_traysh_
4	**quarto**	_kwartoo_
5	**cinco**	_seengkoo_
6	**seis**	_sayeesh_
7	**sete**	_set_
8	**oito**	_oeetoo_
9	**nove**	_nov_
10	**dez**	_desh_
11	**onze**	_ongz_
12	**doze**	_dohz_
13	**treze**	_trayz_
14	**catorze**	_katohrz_
15	**quinze**	_keengz_
16	**dezasseis**	_dezasayeesh_
17	**dezassete**	_dezaset_
18	**dezoito**	_dezoeetoo_
19	**dezanove**	_dezanov_
20	**vinte**	_veengt_
21	**vinte e um**	_veengt e oong_
30	**trinta**	_treengta_
40	**quarenta**	_kwarengta_
50	**cinquenta**	_seengkwengta_
60	**sessenta**	_sessengta_
70	**setenta**	_setengta_
80	**oitenta**	_oeetengta_
90	**noventa**	_noovengta_
100	**cem**	_seng_
1000	**mil**	_meel_
1st	**primeiro/a**	_preemayeeroo/a_
2nd	**segundo/a**	_segoongdoo/a_
3rd	**terceiro/a**	_tersayeeroo/a_
4th	**quarto/a**	_kwartoo/a_
5th	**quinto/a**	_keengtoo/a_

Weights & Measures

gram (=0.03oz)	**grama**	_gram_ma
kilogram (=2.2lb)	**quilograma**	_kee_loogramma
centimetre (=0.4in)	**centímetro**	seng_tee_metroo
metre (=1.1yd)	**metro**	_me_troo
kilometre (=0.6m)	**quilometro**	kee_lo_metroo
litre (=2.1pt)	**litro**	_lee_troo

Days & time

Monday	**segunda-feira**	se_goong_da-_fay_eera
Tuesday	**terça-feira**	_tayr_sa-_fay_eera
Wednesday	**quarta-feira**	_kwar_ta-_fay_eera
Thursday	**quinta-feira**	_keeng_ta-_fay_eera
Friday	**sexta-feira**	_seks_ta-_fay_eera
Saturday	**sábado**	_sab_adoo
Sunday	**domingo**	doo_meeng_oo

What time is it?	**Que horas são?**	k _orash_ saowng?
(Four) o'clock	**(quatro) horas**	(_kwat_roo)_orash_
Quarter past/to (six)	**(seis) e um quarto**	(_say_eesh) e _oong kwar_too
Half past (eight)	**(oito) e meia**	(_oee_too) e _may_eea
Quarter to (ten)	**(dez) menos um quarto**	(desh) _may_noosh _oong kwar_too
morning	**manhã**	man_yang_
afternoon	**tarde**	tard

Clothes size conversions

Women's clothes	34	36	38	40	42	44	46	50
equiv. UK size	6	8	10	12	14	16	18	20

Men's jackets	44	46	48	50	52	54	56	58
equiv. UK size	34	36	38	40	42	44	46	48

Men's shirts	36	37	38	39	40	41	42	43
equiv. UK size	14	14.5	15	15.5	16	16.5	17	17.5

Shoes	36.5	37.5	39	40	41.5	42.5	44	45
equiv. UK size	4	5	6	7	8	9	10	11